THE ABSOLUTE PATH TO SUCCESS
A Great Mentor Can Take You to the Next Level

Tunde Morrow
Co-authored with Raymond Aaron

The Absolute Path to Success: A Great Mentor Can Take You to the Next Level
www.theabsolutepathtosuccess.com
Copyright © 2022 Tunde Morrow

Paperback ISBN: 979-8-4092-1429-6

Publisher
10-10-10 Publishing
Markham, ON   Canada

Printed in Canada and the United States of America

I dedicate this book to my readers,
who inspire me to continue my work
of mentoring others to achieve their dreams.

Table of Contents

Acknowledgments

My special thank you to Raymond Aaron for all of his wisdom and his incredible love for teaching and mentoring. I am also grateful to Raymond for encouraging and motivating me to do and learn more new things in my life. He is a true inspiration.

Grateful acknowledgment to Oprah, even though she doesn't know me.... I am a huge secret admirer of her Super Soul Sunday show on OWN. Every Sunday morning, I get to know two intriguing personalities who talk about books, stories, and other fascinating issues. I especially love when they talk about spiritual things, which led me to many "aha" moments. Thank you, Oprah, for making Sunday morning so beautiful and meaningful for me. All the people who have appeared on the show have greatly impacted my life, including you, Oprah.

I am really grateful to more big personalities: authors like Mary Morrisey, whom I met at her Dream Builder event in Los Angeles, in 2017. The three-day-long dream builder event was a real treat. She talked straight from her soul to convince and encourage people to become successful and live the life they deserve to live.

I am grateful for more highly influential and wildly successful people like Jack Canfield, Bob Proctor, Brian Tracy, T. Harv Eker, and John Assaraf. They have all impacted my life in some way. I learned from them through their work, books, and products.

I am grateful to my husband, Rick, and my son, Andy, who let me be who I am.

For bonuses go to ...

I am so grateful and thankful for Tracy Knepple, who helped me with her amazing talent and skills so that I experienced insight and growth during this journey. It was awesome!

I want to express my gratitude to Gail Lara, a mentor/coach who taught me how to be an entrepreneur. I admire her for her incredible knowledge about business, and for her devotion to her clients.

Other mentors include Madelon Wallace and Barbara Daoust, who have had a great impact on me and expanded my vision by introducing me to Brian Tracy's and Bob Proctor's works.

I am incredibly grateful to Dennis Prager, who is the founder of Prager University. I love his radio show, especially the "Happy Hours." It is very insightful and uplifting. Thank you, Dennis, for sharing your wisdom. You are a living legend!

I am so grateful to Dr. Michael B. Beckwith for his passionate spiritual teaching. you're his presentation entitled "The True Manifestation from the Soul" was magnificent!

I am also thankful to Roger Love for being a wonderful voice coach for me. He is simply the Master of the Voice.

In memory of my loving parent and my sister, Borika.

I am grateful to my closest friends, like Gyorgyi. My friend since preschool, Piroska is my sister too. Gizella was my first best friend in America. These dear friends include Agnes from Hollywood High School, Ica from the church, and many more, including Alanna, Michelle, Eva, Shelley, Ana, Olgi, and Swetlana.

I am grateful to the Hungarian Church in Tarzana, led by Nt. Paster Jakabffy Zsolt Attila and his wife, Rozsa. I am honored to be in this church with like-minded people. I feel uplifted. Thank you, Zsolt, for teaching our children the Hungarian culture and more.

I am very thankful to Vishen Lakhiani, the founder of Mindvalley. They provide many educational courses with exceptional teachers and authors, including Neale Donald Walsch, Maria Diamond, and many more.

I am grateful for all of the prominent internet coaches, like David and Jennifer Perdew who helped me to learn online business. Also, thank you to Bill and Mara Glazer, as well as Rob and Nick James. You all inspired me to be a better entrepreneur.

Finally, I am thankful for all those who are helping me to create new experiences that shape my life.

Foreword

Are you feeling stuck? Is the fire in your belly just about gone out? If you are in a rut and struggling to achieve your goals, then *The Absolute Path to Success: A Great Mentor Can Take You to the Next Level* is the guide you need to stoke your internal fire. Tunde Morrow shares the benefits that mentors can provide to get you on the right path.

Right from the start, Tunde identifies critical obstacles that you might be facing, and how a mentor can be the tool to overcoming those obstacles or challenges. She also provides guidance regarding finding your *why*, embracing your purpose, and setting goals. *The Absolute Path to Success* is more than just a book focused on mentoring; it provides practical tips and tools that you can implement in your daily life.

With unique stories of how to use mentoring to address issues in your life, you can get inspired to find a mentor of your own. Tunde also provides practical tips to maximize the benefits of your mentoring relationship. In exploring mentorship, Tunde also breaks down how it can impact your personal and professional life, as well as the importance of identifying different mentors based on your current challenges.

The Absolute Path to Success: A Great Mentor Can Take You to the Next Level can serve as the guidebook to mentoring as part of your personal or professional transformation. Her tools can help you to better align yourself with your goals by tapping into the various mentors available to you. If you are ready to make a dramatic change and feed your internal fire, then *The Absolute Path to Success: A Great Mentor Can Take You to the Next Level* is the fuel you need!

Loral Langemeier
The Millionaire Maker

Chapter 1

Do You Have a Burning Desire to Be Successful?

Remember, no more effort is required to aim high in life to demand abundance and prosperity, than is required to accept misery and poverty."
– Napoleon Hill, 1883–1970, Author

Success is a word that has a clear definition in the pages of your favorite dictionary. Yet in real life, that sense of what success means is not so easy to capture. Many of us have a burning desire to be successful, but not necessarily a clear path to get there. That desire for success might burn brightly, motivating us to take chances or make a leap out of our comfort zone, but without a clear definition of what success is, all that effort could be in vain.

When it comes to success, you first have to be clear about what you want success to look like in your life, and then find the resources and opportunities necessary to make it happen. So, what is your definition of success? Let me paint a picture of what is often seen as the classic definition of success in the Western world.

A young child is told to do well in school because the better the grades, the better the opportunity to get into a good college or university. They might also be involved in sports, but the goal is to be the best possible. Set records, get the championship, and never stop trying to be the best. After all, sports are seen as another route to get that higher education, which is seen as critical for success. Then you choose a course of study, one that will allow you to move up in your chosen professional field.

Your time at university is full of choices. There are opportunities to take advantage of for extra training, internships, and more. Everything is geared to giving you the greatest advantage out in the world to make money, be the top of your chosen field, and have the big house, the nice car, the best vacations, and be able to afford to give your children everything that they ask for. Success is defined by what you achieve, by what accolades you can point to, and how much money is in the bank.

Now, perhaps that vision of success is what you find is the source of that burning desire inside of you. On the other hand, your definition of success might be based more on the legacy you leave behind for others, the impression you make on those around you, and how you improve the world for those coming after you.

There are also those that believe success is wrapped up in coming to a greater appreciation of who you are, and exploring the inner mysteries related to our personal purpose and unique skills and talents. No matter how we define success, it still is challenging to achieve without a path to follow. After all, how can you measure whether you have been successful or not, without a set of milestones, a defined path forward that takes you from point A to point B?

A Burning Desire Is Not Enough

One of the biggest challenges I find for individuals who want to be successful, is that they are focused on pursuing another person's vision of what success is. Their decisions are driven by the need to reach that definition of success, regardless of the toll it might take on them personally.

The burning desire to be successful, even if it is not your definition of success, can drive us to make decisions that will potentially lead us down a path that ultimately takes us away from the success that we crave. There are so many ways to be distracted, especially when we lack goals, or the measure of success does not truly align with who we are and the values and beliefs that make up our foundation.

Therefore, instead of letting your burning desire to be successful drive you down one path or another, it is important that you start out by defining what success looks like for you. No matter what it is, you need to have that definition clear in your mind. Once you do, then you can determine the best path to get you there. The truth is, without a destination, most of us have a burning desire that eventually fizzles out because there is nothing to fuel it. Success is often defined by the dreams that we have for ourselves and our loved ones, and the type of life that we want to live. Those dreams serve as fuel for us to keep moving forward to achieve that dream, turning it into a reality.

Part of my personal journey has been the realization that a burning desire is useless if it has no purpose and no path to follow to achieve its goals. Time and again, the most motivated individuals in the world have found themselves stuck, and with a burning desire to succeed but no target to aim all that toward.

When I talk about your burning desire, I recognize that it is an energy that must be channeled toward a goal in order for you to find the success of your dreams. My work is wrapped around the idea that without the tools to channel your energy, or burning desire, your dreams will remain unrealized, and all your hard work and effort will be wasted. Why? Simply put, you lack direction, so all that you are doing in an attempt to achieve any form of success, ends up having limited results at best—or worse, no results at all.

Alright, you might be thinking to yourself, *I follow that so far. But I have a set of goals. I have defined a path to my definition of success. What more do I need?*

Many of us love the movies, or to curl up with an amazing fiction tale. There is something amazing about watching the hero start their journey, knowing where they have to go and having the determination to achieve it. Yet at some point in every story and on every journey, there is a moment when the hero falters. They doubt their ability, question the value of what they are doing, and wonder if the choices made to that point were the right ones.

At this moment of crisis for our hero, there comes along a mentor, someone with the wisdom of experience and knowledge, who can give our hero the necessary boost to keep going. They might give the hero important facts, or simply share an inspiring tale. That mentor might be someone who has journeyed that path before, which is encouragement that you can make it to the end and enjoy the rewards of your efforts. That mentor can serve to stoke the burning desire of our hero to succeed.

I would argue that the mentor is a critical part of the story. They find the hero during moments of doubt and fear, and gift them with a shot of motivation, courage, and insight. No hero can make it successfully to their goal without that mentor. Without them, the hero would falter and find themselves giving up, often just short of the prize they have fought so hard to obtain.

When I talk with individuals who are blessed with an amazing burning desire to succeed and achieve their goals, I notice they also find themselves at crossroads during their journey. They might question whether all the effort and sacrifice is worth what they are hoping to achieve. Perhaps you too have felt the same way. The struggles, the sacrifices, and all the effort are starting to weigh you down. You might even begin to question the goals you put in front of yourself, wondering if they are worth it.

At those critical moments in time, when we are faced with struggles or challenges that are making it difficult to reach our dreams or achieve our goals, it is in those moments that we need something more. We need a hero of our own: someone to provide guidance, hope, motivation, or just a healthy dose of understanding; that person who will cheer us on, help us to get up when we fall, and be there to prod us to keep going, knowing that the success we crave is in sight.

You are the hero of your life. Early on, you decided to follow the crowd, or you opted for a different path. Whatever you decided was your dream, your goal, or your version of success, you were determined to go after it. The burning fire inside was all the motivation that you needed. Then you faced that first obstacle. It was challenging, but you figured out how to get through it and you kept moving. However, you might have noticed that your burning desire was not blazing quite as brightly as before. Never mind, you were on the path to achieving your goal. Success would soon follow and taste as sweet as you believed it to be.

Then another obstacle arose, and another. Every time you overcame it and kept moving forward, your burning desire got tamped down a bit more. Over time, you might find that your desire, which was such a critical source of motivation, was now running out. In fact, it was in danger of dying out, and you were in danger of giving up altogether. Right now, in that moment of frustration, when you are tired and so ready to give up, that is when you need the intervention of someone who understands where you are in your journey.

It is the moment when you need your mentor to step in and give you the boost you need, to rekindle that burning desire and to keep you moving forward. Throughout these chapters, my goal is to help you understand how having a mentor can benefit you on your journey to achieve success, and how they can help you get crystal clear about what success looks like, as well as how you might actually be stopping yourself from achieving the success you crave so badly.

Are You Creating Obstacles?

Depending on where you are in your journey toward success as you have defined it, you may be finding that your path is not as clear as it was in the beginning. Situations in your life may have begun to change. Perhaps obstacles that you did not foresee have come up. Now you have reached the point where the path forward is no longer as straightforward as it once was.

Distractions are also constantly around us. It can be easy to follow a sideroad, only to look up later and find we have drifted significantly off course. The obstacles we sought to avoid in the past might have crept into our lives, or we might even have invited them in. Think of your relationships and how they might be helping or hindering your ability to achieve your definition of success.

Often, the everyday challenges of life become the distractions. We get focused on them to the point that they become obstacles. It is possible that we can actually be the ones creating obstacles in our own lives. However, seeing how we might be getting in our own way can be difficult to determine. After all, our focus can be knocked askew by events outside of our control.

Over time, all of these types of distractions can end up dampening your burning desire to achieve your purpose or dreams. After a certain point, you may decide it is no longer worth it, and you may opt to give up. That is when you need someone to step into your path and give you a boost. That person might have a significant relationship with you or just be a person you have recently met, but the end result is that their help will be invaluable to your journey.

Think back to our hero in that fiction story. As part of the hero's journey, there may have been distractions that got our hero off course. They might have been the advice of others or even appealing opportunities that seemed to take him closer to the goal. Yet in the end, they were all distractions that kept our hero from his true journey. To progress, he needed to get rid of those distractions and get back on his path. It might require making changes—some significant ones—particularly in attitude, skills, or allies. Yet the end result is that the hero reached his goal.

Like our hero, you might have gotten distracted by the everyday aspects of life, or even the challenges that have started to feel like overwhelming obstacles. As a result, you too might have strayed off of the path and now be struggling to find your way forward. Now that struggle could leave you feeling as if you are simply spinning your wheels, making no progress at all. That can contribute to feelings of frustration, helping them to grow even more, and thus begins a cycle of frustration that drives you even further off course.

How many ways can we be delayed? One is by outside experiences or circumstances. There can be so much going on that it becomes a source of frustration, because we cannot give our attention to our purpose. It is also possible to get sidetracked by relationships or the advice of others that our course is not appropriate. Doubting our own judgment can also end up being an obstacle that makes it difficult for us to stay on our path. Each of these things can end up feeding a cycle of frustration.

In order to move yourself past this cycle of frustration, and to get back on track, like our hero, you may have to take some pretty drastic steps. However, it can be difficult to know what steps you need to take. The situation you find yourself in can be clouding your vision. A mentor, much like the one our hero found, can be a way to clear your vision and give you the means to get back on track, thus breaking your cycle of frustration.

In the next few chapters, we will take a journey to discover the different obstacles that you might be facing, and how they are serving to distract you or smother your burning desire. Your purpose might have disappeared temporarily from view and, as a result, your fire has become just a few flickering flames. I will share a few stories of how individuals used mentors to stoke their desire and inspire them to keep moving forward to achieve their goals, no matter the obstacles.

As we define a few of these obstacles, I will also outline some ways that you can get unstuck, get back on track, and rekindle your burning desire to achieve success. That involves more than just outlining a few milestones, or vaguely outlining what success means to you. It involves giving yourself a clear path, while recognizing that flexibility is necessary when dealing with different challenges or obstacles.

If you are still full of that burning desire, and are clear on what your definition of success is, then these chapters will help you to prepare for potential obstacles. The truth is that all of us are driven by a purpose, and once you discover what that purpose is, then you can understand your path and what you need to do to achieve that purpose. Your burning desire can serve as the fuel you need.

Along the way, like our hero, you will also discover mentors. They will serve as guides, signposts, and the means to feed your fire when necessary. There are so many ways that a mentor can assist you and provide a soundboard for reconnecting with your purpose.

This journey is not about you finding your purpose, so much as it is about keeping yourself on track to fulfill it and reach your definition of success. It is not always an easy process, and doing it on our own can be challenging to the point that you might even feel as if you are ready to give up.

Let's get started in defining those obstacles, and outlining how they can negatively impact your burning desire to succeed.

Chapter 2

Are You Facing Obstacles in Reaching Your Dreams?

*"At the end of the day, we are accountable to ourselves.
Our success is the result of what we do."*
– Catherina Pulsifer, Author

Your burning desire to achieve a purpose has likely been fueling your dreams. Those dreams might be focused on what you want to achieve in your life, how you want to live as you get older, or even how you want to create your family. The point is that having a dream can be a driving force to keep you motivated to do the work to achieve it. However, no matter what your dreams are, or the goals you have put into place to see it come to fruition, the truth is that obstacles can pop up.

Those obstacles might be ones that we create ourselves or ones that circumstances have put into our path. In this chapter, I want to identify a few of those obstacles and some of the ways that you can deal with them to keep making progress toward your dreams, instead of getting sidetracked. Let's start by identifying a common obstacle, often known as distraction.

Are You Distracted?

When you have a dream and a goal, it can be exciting. You are eager to work hard to achieve it. Yet when the dream is going to take years to achieve, it can be challenging to remain focused. Life has a way of bringing distractions into every aspect of our lives. Society now rewards being busy, even if the things we are busy doing are actually keeping us from achieving our goals.

Distractions can end up creating a rut, one that moves us into the position of elevating the mundane aspects of our lives.

Tara had the goal of running her own business, helping others to implement environmentally friendly shopping processes by creating a high-quality reusable market bag from recycled materials. She developed her product, but then her family started to grow, and her focus turned to building a professional career that would bring in a steady paycheck. She vowed to keep working on her business in the evenings, but then there were school activities, sports, and so many things that had to be done to keep her family going.

Several years went by, and Tara unearthed that original prototype. She wondered what had happened to her idea and focus. It seemed that her day was filled with going to work, making money for someone else, and then rushing home to meet the demands of her family. She was left feeling frustrated and sad.

A friend recommended a mentor, and Tara decided to make time for these short meetings. Amazingly enough, her mentor was able to target areas where Tara had gotten into a rut, allowing routine to steal away time that could be devoted to her dreams. That perspective is what Tara needed, to make some major changes.

It can be challenging to see when we have become distracted, or to define the root cause of our distractions. Often, the first thing we need to do is sit down and clearly set out our goals. Then we need to examine our daily schedule. Is that schedule helping us to reach our goals and dreams faster? The truth is that you may find that your schedule is actually working against you, as the mundane or busy lifestyle is taking time away from what is truly important to you.

That being said, once you evaluate your daily schedule and routine, you might identify things that are simply time fillers or busyness without a purpose. Eliminate those items. That might mean saying no to some individuals, or letting go of a hectic social schedule. In the end, you are reclaiming your time and energy, thus being in a position to refocus that on your priorities.

When you get to the point that your schedule has overshadowed your goals and dreams, then it is time for a shift and a meaningful change. The challenge is finding ways to break away from the distractions and return your focus to what really matters to you.

Part of the challenge in getting past distractions is learning how to identify distractions early on. Routines and habits can become so normal that we are not aware of how they are allowing distractions to creep in until it is too late. Therefore, I encourage individuals to practice mindfulness when it comes to their routine. Do not just go through the day on autopilot. Instead, employ mindfulness throughout the day, asking yourself critical questions about your different activities. That awareness can assist you in identifying when you might be losing your focus, and help you to get reoriented in the direction you want to go.

Mindfulness can also be a critical part of your decision-making process when determining if you will take responsibility for a new project, or add another social obligation to your schedule. Consider whether it will add something to your life or if it will help to move you closer to fulfilling your purpose. That can help you to avoid distractions by not mindlessly obligating yourself in the first place.

Still, distractions are not the only challenges that you will face as you work toward achieving a dream.

The Impact of Limiting Beliefs

All of us have a specific set of beliefs that govern how we live and the decisions we make. Those beliefs often are first created in childhood, where our parents, extended family, and friends bring their input and influence into our lives. Society also begins to shape our beliefs as we grow into young adults. Those beliefs then become the basis for how we view our experiences and the knowledge we have gained. Essentially, those beliefs become the filter or lens through which we understand our world, and governs the judgments that we make.

While it can seem that our beliefs are concrete and stay with us forever, the truth is that our beliefs can be changed. Experiences and new information can put us in the position of reevaluating what we believe and why we believe it. Change is possible, but it requires effort on our part.

The challenge for some of us is that our current set of beliefs can be rather limiting. They might steer us away from anything that could be perceived as risk or even just a small step outside of our comfort zone. The overriding need to be safe means that we tell ourselves that things are not possible for us, just to avoid any potential hurt or risk.

Mentally, that can translate into other challenges. Our limiting beliefs might throw up all the reasons why we cannot achieve a particular goal, focusing on how we are not good enough, or other negative aspects. The result is that you end up with a constant thought process geared toward not taking risks, not believing in your own capabilities and powers, and thus living with a fear of failure. That fear keeps you from ever taking the steps necessary to achieve your purpose and make your dreams a reality.

It is not always easy to figure out when your limiting beliefs are kicking in, but it is critical to examine why you are making certain choices. On the surface, those choices might appear reasonable, based on certain circumstances or facts. Yet once you dig a little deeper, you can find the real reason or belief that is guiding your thought process.

Now when you ferret out one of your beliefs, you have to put it to the test. Determine if it is still serving you or if it is a belief that is limiting your potential. Working with different individuals, I find they are amazed at how often they have been limiting themselves through the beliefs that they held, and they did not even realize it.

Examining your beliefs is like holding up a mirror in front of yourself. It gives you a chance to honestly look at your foundation and address problem areas. After all, when you look in the mirror, you are checking to make sure your clothes look alright, your hair is in place, and any accessories are just right. If you notice something is not in the right place, then you can make adjustments before you leave the house.

When you dive into your beliefs, you are giving yourself that same opportunity to make adjustments as necessary, to bring your best self to your life and relationships. Often, it is not easy to see how our beliefs could be limiting us, but the truth is that all of us have some beliefs that no long serve us. Determining what ones need to change is part of our growth and a critical aspect of achieving our dreams.

Do You Fear Failure?

All of us have had moments in our lives when we failed. It happened because we were not prepared, the decisions in front of us were not well thought out, or someone simply was better than we were at whatever it was. The truth is that failing does not mean you are a failure. It simply means you did not achieve your goal this time. That is not a reflection of who you are. Unfortunately, it can be easy for us to tie our self-worth to our success or failure in a given situation.

Professionally, you might wonder if you will ever achieve your goals. Your internal dialogue can start to attack your self-confidence, making you doubt your capabilities and talents. Then you start making more mistakes, reinforcing that negative self-talk. It becomes a nasty habit that can leave you mired in your failures, instead of learning from them and allowing them to help you find the path to success.

Breaking that habit is key to embracing failure. Why would I tell you to embrace failure? Simply put, failure is a great learning opportunity. It gives you a chance for self-reflection, to evaluate your decisions and actions in the light of the results, and then make adjustments. As humans, we are not meant to be in a static place, never moving or changing. We are meant to be on a path of growth.

Everything that happens in our lives is a chance to learn, change, and improve. There is no such thing as reaching perfection. Learning, growing, and changing are a natural part of the human condition. Often, to benefit from failure, the first thing that we need to do is shift our viewpoint. See failure as part of growth. In fact, you might find it helpful to stop referring to it as failure, but simply seeing it as eliminating one option and thus freeing you to explore others.

Thomas Edison, who spent years trying to create a lightbulb, once said, "I have not failed. I've just found 10,000 ways that won't work." Later, he also spoke about weakness in a way that perfectly frames how our view of failure can impact our ability to move forward. "Our greatest weakness lies in giving up. The most certain way to succeed is always to try just one more time," said Edison.

How do you view failure? That viewpoint is going to be the key to reaching success or finding yourself giving up. As I work with people focusing on personal and professional growth, I find that those who see failures as a way to improve, ultimately find the success they seek. Their talents and unique abilities are put to use, and they find great joy in achieving their dreams and working for their purpose.

Not Having Clear Goals

As I discussed in the first chapter, you can have a burning desire to achieve something, only to find yourself frustrated because you lack a sense of direction. You may even know what you want to achieve, but without a clear path forward, then it can be challenging to achieve it. Creating a set of goals and milestones provide that path, giving you the ability to achieve your goals.

That being said, milestones mean nothing without a timeframe. What type of timeframe works best? It needs to be realistic. In other words, if you are looking to lose 30 pounds, then you should not have your goal to be 10 pounds in 3 days. That is not a realistic timeframe. Therefore, it is important to create timeframes that reflect a reasonable schedule for completing different milestones.

On the other hand, you do not want to make those timeframes so broad that there is no incentive for you to achieve anything related to your milestones and long-term goals. Let's face it; as humans, deadlines have a way of driving us to get focused and achieve. They can assist us in overcoming another challenge, which is procrastination. Essentially, deadlines can keep you from putting off what is necessary for you to accomplish. They can also be a way to avoid putting yourself in a bind later, as you try to keep promises that you have made to yourself and others.

Therefore, milestones and goals need a clear and reasonable timeframe in order to be effective and keep you on track to achieving your purpose, dreams, or desires.

Procrastination Blocks Your Progress

Ally had a reputation for arriving at the last minute in every aspect of her life. If you made plans with her for the weekend, she was late. If you were working with her, then her part of the project would be finalized at the last minute. Although she produced quality work, because of the rushing she did at the end, mistakes could creep in and cost time and money.

Her constant procrastination negatively impacted her relationships. Many individuals opted not to make plans with her because everything was so last minute. Ally started to notice that she was not achieving her goals. She felt stuck but was not sure what needed to change. Her mentor was able to target her procrastination. By working on strategies with her, Ally was able to start making real progress, both professionally and personally.

No matter who you are, there have been moments in your life when you have procrastinated. In the simplest terms, procrastination is putting off difficult or time-consuming tasks. However, procrastination can have a negative effect on your ability to make progress in your life if it becomes a chronic habit. Some people argue that chronic procrastination demonstrates a lack of self-control, thus feeding negative feelings that further encourage the procrastination behaviors.

On some level, procrastination does involve awareness of how putting things off is negatively impacting their goals, relationships, and more, but the idea of changing habits can be overwhelming. Perhaps you have dealt with procrastination in different areas of your life. While you might think it shows

19

you have a lack of self-control, it also could be a sign that you are such a perfectionist that never starting something is better than not being able to do it perfectly.

Another reason for procrastination is the belief that pressure enhances performance. You might have a few instances where that has been the case. Overall, when you work in a constant state of waiting for the last-minute rush, critical details can be missed, and the quality of your work suffers.

There are multiple drivers that can lead you down the path of procrastination, such as low self-confidence, anxiety, lack of structure, and a lack of motivation. Clearly, it can be a self-defeating behavior. I find that there are few ways to combat procrastination in your daily life. First, create a schedule and use it throughout the day. You might find that it is hard to keep to that schedule at first, but after a few weeks, that schedule will become a habit and give you the structure necessary to avoid procrastinating.

Secondly, I encourage people to find someone to be accountable to for completing tasks in a timely manner. Mentors can serve as that source of accountability and motivation to stick with your schedule.

Third, you want to avoid potential distractions. How many of us have been working on a task and stopped to check our phone, only to find hours have gone by as we got caught up in checking emails and social media? While it is important to take breaks, set a timer to remind yourself to get back on task.

Fourth, break up a big job into smaller tasks that seem less overwhelming. Doing that can give you the motivation to get started, combatting the feeling of being overwhelmed. As part of this, I encourage you to take the time to celebrate when you do complete something. That can fuel your excitement to keep moving forward, and will keep your momentum up.

Finally, recognize that you are still going to procrastinate from time to time. It is not an easy habit to break. Therefore, as you build your schedule, make sure to build some time for any delays. It can relieve some of the pressure as you start to learn your new schedule. However, as a word of caution, you should not focus on that extra delay time, because it can easily become an excuse for continued procrastination.

Throughout this section, the focus has been on defining procrastination, what might be driving your procrastination, and some practical steps to combat it. Underneath all of that, however, is your mindset. While you might benefit right now from putting something off, your future self is now being put under pressure. If you shift your mindset to focusing on how you can help your future self, then it can make the process of shifting away from procrastination easier.

Shifting your mindset is not always easy, but it is definitely worth the effort. Now, perhaps your procrastination comes into play when you are trying to make decisions. If that is the case, then it can benefit from creating a set of decision-making rules. These rules are much like a computer program, where if one situation presents itself, then you would choose A instead of B. While it might not work for every situation, a set of decision-making rules can be a way to take the pressure off and make it easier to handle decisions that fall outside of your set rules.

Clearly, there are multiple obstacles that can make it challenging to reach your goals or achieve your purpose. Plus, it is not like these obstacles come up one at a time. In fact, they frequently come in groups, making it even more challenging to keep your drive and internal fire burning.

Often, if you are facing multiple obstacles or challenges at the same time, then you can be tempted to give up. At those moments, you need more than just a schedule or a mindset shift. You need a fresh perspective and someone who will tell you what you need to hear. With that in mind, let's talk about the benefits of having a mentor.

Chapter 3

Getting Help From a Mentor!

"One's destination is never a place, but a new way of seeing things."
– Henry Miller

n each of the challenges presented in Chapter 2, I focused on how you can overcome them. Still, that can be difficult if you are depending on your own unique point of view. As we discussed, our viewpoint can be clouded by our limiting beliefs, our view of failure, procrastination, and even the opinions of others.

Breaking through all of those challenges can often be more than we can tackle on our own. With that in mind, the focus needs to shift away from how we tackle these challenges on our own, to how you can tap into resources that will support, motivate, hold you accountable, and keep you focused and on track. What fits the bill? A mentor!

Still, you might be wondering what a mentor is. Typically, it is an individual acting as an advisor for someone who is less experienced or advanced. Their expertise and professional knowledge come with a seasoned perspective. Essentially, you are connecting with someone who has already been where you are right now, and their guidance can be critical for you to reach your next level of personal and professional growth.

Finding the Right Support Through a Mentor

At the core of the relationship, a mentor provides a level of support for you throughout transitions in your life. That support also comes from a place of caring about your best interests. Providing support might actually involve a level of tough love. What does that look like? They can look from outside of the situation and identify the ways that you might be actually sabotaging yourself.

When I spoke of the different obstacles and challenges in the previous chapter, it became apparent to me that you might not be able to identify how you are standing in your way. After all, your focus is just on moving forward and working hard to reach your goals. Yet all that work and effort could end up just being wasted, simply because you are not making any measurable progress. Imagine how that could contribute to your level of frustration and really dampen your internal fire and drive.

Therefore, having a mentor can be a way to provide a different point of view, one that can assist in identifying critical obstacles, and even giving you tips on how to address them. That does not mean you are entirely dependent on the mentor for decision making. Instead, they serve as a unique resource, particularly when your progress is slowed in one area or another.

There are also concrete benefits you can enjoy from a mentor relationship. For instance, you might be striving for a new professional opportunity. A mentor can provide a reference, focusing on the skills, knowledge, and experience that you can bring to your next job or position. They can also be a resource of practical professional advice, particularly about career moves that could be advantageous versus ones that might have only limited benefits. When you spend time with your mentor, you are challenged to think differently, to employ critical thinking skills, and to analyze your long-term professional development. Notice that such an analysis can be key to establishing goals or milestones that can contribute to your long-term development of leadership skills or more concrete knowledge that increases your abilities, thus allowing you to take on greater professional roles.

While mentors can be a critical aspect of your professional development, they can also play a significant role in your personal development as well. Mentors can be individuals you regularly interact with, or they can provide knowledge and practical wisdom through books, podcasts, or lectures. The point is that by tapping into mentors in various areas of your life, you can see the practical benefits.

Now let's talk about the different types of mentors that you can tap into, both personally and professionally.

The Different Types of Mentors

There was a college student named Anna, who was unsure about her career path. She knew that she wanted to join the medical field but was not comfortable with needles or blood. Still, she had enrolled in the nursing program at her college because she was determined to help people when they were sick and vulnerable. To achieve that dream, a form of medical school seemed the only way forward.

A professor noticed that Anna was struggling in the practical application of what she was learning, especially when it came to taking blood samples or even the simulations of injuries. Taking Anna aside, she started asking questions, getting to know Anna, not just as a student but as an individual. Not surprisingly, as she did, this professor was also able to see areas where Anna's organizational skills, and her ability to quickly figure out the issues with the class computers, meant that medical IT would likely be a much better fit. Having a heart-to-heart with Anna was the next step, and although it was hard to hear that nursing school was not right for her, Anna appreciated the practical advice. After changing her major, Anna went on to a successful career, building software for medical clinics and hospitals.

This example showed that mentors can be found in all areas of your life. In this case, Anna found a mentor in her professor, one that was able to identify areas where Anna excelled, thus allowing her to have a career in the medical field, but one that tapped into her talents.

Too often, our biggest obstacle can be that we see only one way to achieve a dream, not recognizing all the different possibilities available. Mentors can provide a way for us to explore different options and thus break out of a narrow point of view that limits our options to just option A or option B. Too often, that narrow point of view can stop us from seeing the other options, such as Option C, Option D, or more. When you feel that it is an either/or situation, then that is when a mentor's point of view can be the most critical.

However, not every mentor is exactly the same or right for every situation. Let's explore what types of mentors there are available, and how they can provide valuable assistance.

Peer mentors – These are professional colleagues that can advise you. Companies might set up a peer mentor program for new employees, allowing you to spend time with someone who knows your new job and can provide guidance on company culture. They interact with you, perhaps checking in on a regular basis, along with spending time with you in formal meetings and social settings. While they might be a great way to help you get acclimated to a new company or position, the truth is that these peer mentors are often limited in the assistance they can provide.

Career mentors – These individuals are often higher up the professional ladder, thus being in a position to serve as both advocates and guides. They can share with you how to progress based on your current role. At the same time, a career mentor can let you know if you might be in a position with limited growth opportunities. You might find that your career mentor does not check in as frequently, but they are still available when needed. You might find that they are part of your current company in a different department, or could even be a manager. On the other hand, a career mentor could also be just a part of the industry.

Life mentors – Professionally, these individuals might have reached the point where they are ready for retirement. They provide a wealth of wisdom and experience, which can be tapped during difficult moments of your life, either in your personal life or career. Think of them as the means to tap into an unbiased point of view, particularly in challenging situations. You can also tap into their experience and knowledge to make critical decisions, either to change your professional or personal direction.

Clearly, there are plenty of instances where mentors can be helpful, even if it is just for a short period of time or over an extended period. The truth is that mentors can play a pivotal role in our progress toward a goal or the fulfillment of a dream. While mentors are often thought of more frequently in terms of our professional development, the truth is that mentors can be used in all areas of our lives.

Think about how you might have goals in fitness, health, and relationships, and in personal, professional, or spiritual growth. A mentor for fitness might not be the best to inform you about your professional goals. Likewise, your professional mentor might not be the best person to inform you about your spiritual goals, or share techniques regarding personal growth. As I will discuss later, mentorship in different areas of your life can be a vital part of your growth as a whole person, particularly as you identify areas where you might be lacking, or uncover different weaknesses.

With a greater understanding of what mentors can do, and the types of mentors that can be found, let's dive into how you can make the most of these relationships.

How to Be the Best Mentee

Mentors can provide us so much, but it is also interesting that even as we are being mentored, we can serve as a mentor to someone else. The beauty of mentoring is that it is fundamentally based on helping others, sharing knowledge, and giving constructive criticism or advice where appropriate. These relationships are so vital to who we are and how we grow that they cannot be easily dismissed or disregarded.

However, if you are in a position of being a mentee, then you want to get the most out of the relationship. The question is how to do so without overwhelming your mentor or becoming so demanding that they want to end the relationship. Here are a few tips that I have found critical to enjoying a mutually beneficial mentor-mentee relationship.

First, you need to recognize that this relationship is not one-sided. While you might be gleaning a wealth of information from your mentor, they are also gaining a fresh perspective from you. What you share with them could end up being vital to their understanding of your challenges, and could help them to filter their advice to be more personally applicable.

Still, you can also do much to make it an enjoyable experience for the both of you. It is not like a classroom, where you simply sit and take a lot of notes. There is a give and take, but if you are taking only, the relationship can simply

29

stall out. You have to give of yourself so that your mentor is encouraged to keep working with you.

To get the most out of your mentorship, start by being engaged and showing an interest in what they have to offer. Doing so will help your mentor feel as if you understand the value of their time and respect it. Also, ask them questions about themselves. Get to know them. Recognize that even if you do not take every suggestion offered by your mentor, you chose them for a reason. Consider carefully what they have said and the guidance that they offer.

When you follow the advice of your mentor, then you demonstrate that you value the relationship and their experience. They also can see that you take the experience seriously, which can be encouraging to your mentor and make them more likely to continue guiding you beyond the initial season of your relationship.

Practice taking and applying it to your particular situation. The reality is that you might find yourself arguing with your mentor, pointing out why their advice will not work in your situation. That is the narrow point of view, which I have discussed previously as an obstacle to your growth. Getting honest feedback and constructive criticism can be beneficial, but only if you are willing to be open to accepting it. Essentially, you need to turn off your natural desire to make excuses, and instead foster a mindset that can allow for different ideas and thoughts to flourish.

Another benefit of taking advice and accepting feedback can be that you identify different strengths that you were not aware of, as well as weaknesses that could be hindering your personal and professional progress.

Remember that your mentor is not just sitting around waiting for you to call or visit with them. They have other obligations and goals of their own. Be respectful of their time, and do not contact them excessively. Also, when you are spending time with them, have questions ready or specific topics that you want to cover. The goal is to maximize the benefits of your time with them, while making sure that they recognize that you respect their efforts on your behalf.

Finding the Best Mentors for You

Clearly, the benefits of mentors cannot be understated. However, just because someone is an authority in an industry or one area, does not necessarily mean that they will be the right fit for you. Therefore, you want to look for some key indicators that will help determine if this mentoring relationship will work for you.

First, look for compatibility. That does not mean you both will agree on everything, but having a connection with your mentor can make it easier to hear things that challenge your beliefs or current point of view. That compatibility will also make it easier for you to share your struggles and unique challenges, feeling confident in the relationship that your concerns can stay private.

Secondly, you want a mentor who provides diverse perspectives. After all, if you find someone with a similar background to your own, and similar perspectives, it can be hard for you to get the full benefit of the mentor relationship. Those diverse backgrounds and points of view give you a new perspective that can allow you to make the best option possible.

Michael worked with a mentor who was not from his home country. Their backgrounds were very different, as well as their unique cultural experiences. At first, Michael did not think he could get anything out of the relationship. However, he kept going, keeping an open mind. As he did, his mentor shared unique examples that helped Michael to evaluate his professional career. Later, Michael shared that this mentor relationship was a turning point for him professionally, opening the door to opportunities.

Along the way, you need to build a level of trust with your mentor. Trust is critical if you are going to be willing to take their advice and make decisions based on the information and perspective that they share. A level of connection can take time to develop, but if you do not feel you could grow to trust your mentor, then the connection will never successfully develop. Mutual respect is also a critical ingredient to a successful mentor-mentee relationship.

Finally, expertise is important, but do not dismiss a potential mentor just because they are not at the top of their field or industry. Instead, look for specific experience or skills that can benefit you, particularly if their strengths are areas in which you might have identified personal weaknesses.

After you share your concerns with your mentor, be prepared to listen with an open mind and heart. Your mentor offers you multiple benefits, as well as providing you the chance to take advantage of opportunities that you might not have known about. Your mentor is a conduit for connection, with people who can also provide knowledge and experience.

While you are the primary beneficiary from the mentor-mentee relationship, the mentor also benefits from the opportunity to learn from you. It can be a truly mutual beneficial relationship.

Still, a mentor is only beneficial if you know your purpose and the "why" behind all of your efforts. In the next chapter, the focus is finding out the reason behind your burning desire to achieve your definition of success. Let's get started!

Chapter 4

Knowing Your Why As Part of Finding Your Purpose

"When I let go of what I am, I become what I might be."
– Lau Tzu, Philosopher

For many of us, the fire within, that driving desire, is key to motivating us and keeping us on track to achieve our goals and dreams. Yet there is the challenge that comes when we try to keep that fire burning bright. Initially, how we benefit from our actions can be enough fuel for that internal fire. Over time, that self-serving aspect will not be enough of a driver. As human beings, our basic need is to define our purpose in life and then do our best to fulfill it.

That search for purpose can end up lasting a lifetime. Yet some individuals are able to determine their purpose fairly early in life, and their goals are aligned with this larger purpose. Everything that they do is meant to drive them toward achieving that purpose.

On the other hand, there are individuals who spend a portion of their life trying to find that "why," the reason and purpose behind their goals and dreams. To find their why or purpose, some individuals start by exploring their talents. As they do so, it exposes them to opportunities where they can use those talents fully, in the service of others or to contribute to the greater good of their communities.

Perhaps you are struggling to find your purpose. You might have a significant desire to succeed, but you are struggling to define exactly what you want to succeed at! There are individuals who focus all their talents and efforts on reaching professional goals, wanting to be the top in their field. The idea is that they will be successful if their bank account reaches a certain point, they have a specific title at their company, and people treat them with awe.

However, those that have achieved that type of success do not always find that it is as fulfilling as advertised. At some point, they begin to recognize that their success is not necessarily wrapped up in material possessions or professional accolades. As a result, they start to question if this is all there is, or if they really have another purpose, one that contributes to others in a significant way.

This situation actually reminds me of an individual who found and runs a charity that helps communities get access to clean water. He had achieved what could have been defined as the ultimate dream career, organizing parties and becoming a social media influencer when the trend was still fresh. Yet he ended up reaching a point where he knew that a change was necessary. During a volunteer trip with another organization, which provided medical care to individuals with facial deformities, he learned that many of these communities lacked access to sources of clean water. He saw firsthand how that impacted the ability of children to get an education, how families were limited in how much income they could create, and how illness was more prevalent due to water borne disease and bacteria. His focus in life changed. All the talents he had employed, getting people to show up at parties and events in exchange for money, were now being deployed to help him raise money to dig wells. Today, he runs a non-profit known as Charity Water. His children are being raised with the ideals of providing this basic necessity so that families and communities can thrive.

Notice how his purpose did not speak out to him initially, but that he found his purpose during a trip to realign himself, which ultimately became the turning point in his life. The work that he does is not easy, but it is satisfying because his purpose is based in something greater than himself.

Why did I share this story? Perhaps because I understand that when we reach out for mentors, it can be to help us in the journey to find our purpose by eliminating what does not work for us. Mentors have a way of cutting through all the excuses and all the reasons we create to not pursue our dreams in the most authentic way possible. They help us to get clear about what we

www.theabsolutepathtosuccess.com

are good at, what we can contribute to others, and assist us in finding practical ways to do just that.

It is not easy to find a way to fulfill your purpose, yet for some of us, getting there is half the fun. Exploring the world and getting to know people around the globe can be an enriching experience, one that can end up exposing you to the right opportunity to identify and pursue your purpose.

If you are unsure of your purpose or why, then spend some time talking with your mentor. Ask how they identified their purpose and what the different things were that they focused on during their search. You may be surprised at how much your mentor can assist you in this unique process. Let's begin by exploring a few questions that you can ask yourself as part of this journey to discover your why, which can fuel your desire to achieve it.

Questions to Find the Sweet Spot

When you first start the journey to find your purpose, it often helps to gain a deeper understanding of who you are and what makes you special. Doing so will be a critical part in defining the unique contribution that you can make in the world. The world today is dealing with a crisis that comes from a lack of purpose and meaning in our lives. Being well-off financially is not necessarily the same as your well-being, mentally, emotionally, physically, and spiritually.

"He who has a 'why' to live can bear almost any 'how,'" said Frederick Nietzsche, a German philosopher. Fundamentally, if you have a why, then it can help you decide how to achieve the goals that fulfill the why. You create a life that excites you, and one you enjoy. That "why" can also give you the courage to take risks, stay motivated during difficult moments, and thus move your life into a new direction, one you might not have initially envisioned.

With that in mind, there are a few questions that you should take some time to contemplate as you determine your why. The first question is wrapped around what inspires you. The point is to gain a deeper insight into what makes you unique, and a better understanding of what frames your decisions, as well as your values and beliefs. Your life's work, your purpose, and your "why" are often at the intersection of your passions, values, skills, talents, and expertise.

What makes you come alive? When you are working to achieve things that inspire you, it makes you feel alive and excited to get up every day. I am not talking about a dream vacation or getting to watch your favorite entertainer live; it is something that is so much bigger. Fundamentally, it is when something moves beyond being just about you, and becomes something more. This question is about identifying what you are passionate about, what influences you in ways that nothing else ever does or has, and what truly fuels the fire in your belly. It is about connecting with a bigger cause, but one that aligns with what you care about and who you are.

Exploring Your Strengths and Contributions

Now let's dive into your strengths. When you describe yourself to others, are there natural talents and skills that you automatically include? The passion or what makes you come alive is going to meet up with these innate strengths, creating an amazing place where you are at your best. In those moments, you are productive, adding value, and enjoying fulfillment, either professionally or personally. Your talents could be in communication, creativity, innovation, or organization. You might be able to quickly determine the solution to a puzzle, or are mechanically inclined.

No matter what those talents are, the point is to have them clearly in your mind as you define your purpose. Those strengths might not be immediately evident, but if you take the time to focus on what you enjoy, they will start to make themselves apparent.

"Don't ask yourself what the world needs;
ask yourself what makes you come alive, then go do that.
Because what the world needs is people who have come alive."
– Howard Thurmond, Civil Rights Leader

We all have those things that come to us with ease. You might even wonder why others find it so challenging, when you find it so simple. Our purpose, or "why," can often fall in line with our natural talents. You might be passionate about things that you are not talented at, but more often than not, we tend to aspire or be ambitious for things that utilize our natural talents.

38

Now that you have your talents in mind, let's talk about how you can use those strengths and talents to add value to the world. Adding value involves the application of your education, skills, strengths, knowledge, experience, and abilities, to achieve your goals and purpose. When you think about how you can add value, it gives you focus regarding the opportunities and the paths that can lead you where you want to go.

The problem is that it can be easy to undervalue what you can contribute. However, when you reframe it from the idea of adding value or solving problems, then you can determine if you are in the right place and equipped to handle what is in front of you. That being said, if you find yourself slightly out of your element, use that as the means to motivate yourself to get the skills or experience necessary to help you move forward. See it as taking a risk that can catapult you forward toward achieving your purpose.

Are there problems you enjoy solving? Is there a particular problem that drives you to find a solution? By focusing on your strengths, especially those that come naturally to you, then success will flow in your direction. The problem is that often we tend to focus on bolstering or working on our weaknesses, to the point that we totally ignore the strengths that we have. My point is that while you do not want to ignore your weaknesses, or working on self-improvement, the truth is that by working in harmony with your innate strengths, you will find it easier to identify your "why."

Finally, let's talk about how you measure your life. As I mentioned earlier, success looks and feels different to us all. By deciding how you want to measure your life, you are essentially defining success for yourself, and also making it clear what you stand for. Knowing what you stand for allows you to align your life in accord with your beliefs and values.

Living with purpose is about focusing on what matters to you and letting go of the distractions. The challenge can be that the distractions tend to pose as things that seem as if they align with your purpose. The reality is that what you truly value rarely can be described as a thing. Shifting your lens and how you view what you are doing right now can help you draw meaning and align with your purpose, even if you are still in the process of working toward your goals.

Nathan always wanted to live in another area of the country, but every time he started to make progress toward the goal, it seemed as if something would come up. Working with his mentor, he started to identify the potential roadblocks keeping him from achieving his goal. Nathan also found that he had some bad habits, which were also contributing to his lack of progress. Inspired by what he learned, Nathan made changes and saw real progress. Less than a year later, Nathan had moved and made several leaps professionally. His mentorship had been an eye-opening relationship, helping him to learn more about himself and discover how to make real changes to achieve his goals.

As you spend the time to learn more about yourself, recognize that there is a need for you to take the next step and get inspired by the challenge, instead of allowing those challenges to block you from moving down the path to your purpose. However, you might find it difficult to take the time out for this deeper introspection.

I encourage individuals to schedule quiet time for introspection or meditation. The point is to find time to quiet your mind, allowing you to block out the distractions that can creep up. Are there relationships, both professionally or personally, that have become toxic? When that toxicity happens, it obscures our why, keeping us from focusing on achieving our purpose, because we are completely focused on dealing with that toxicity.

How can a relationship become toxic? One way is when there is a lack of mutual support for each other, especially when it comes to achieving goals. Time and again, toxic relationships can drain us of the energy necessary to successfully reach our goals.

Curing these toxic relationships can be extremely challenging, because our logical and clear point of view can be overclouded by our emotions. Therefore, taking the time for daily introspection and meditation can be the best way to start looking at relationships calmly, thus temporarily removing the emotional response.

It is amazing how calm introspection can also give us to the courage to do what is necessary to cure these relationships and get ourselves back on the path toward achieving our dreams, purpose, and goals. There is a level of connection that you must create with yourself to be right where you need to be as your work brings your legacy to fruition.

My personal journey of growth to reach my purpose of helping others to find their unique path, started by finding my own. I spent time with mentors, ones who could help me to be my best self in all areas of my life. Throughout every stage, as I learned from one mentor, I also saw opportunities to connect with other mentors. While I was identifying my strengths, I saw how my mentors and their strengths could help me to address weaknesses, thus turning them into additional strengths.

You, too, can have a similar experience by tapping into mentors through-out your journey. By starting the process of identifying your purpose and clearly knowing your why, then you can rid yourself of the obstacles in your path. If your vision of your purpose gets blurred, mentors can be a way to help crystalize your vision once again.

With that in mind, let's talk about how a mentor can be a critical part of your journey, thus giving fuel to keep your internal fire burning brightly while you discover your purpose.

Mentoring Yourself to Grow to Your Purpose

Along the journey of finding your purpose and identifying your why, it can be easy to get distracted by the daily tasks of life. Your desire to contribute to something greater than yourself reaches beyond any definition of success, and into the heart of your legacy as an individual. When we talk about mentoring, it often gets focused on the professional aspects of our lives. That means we set goals to achieve professional success but often put our personal success on the back burner. However, by shifting your focus away from just your definition of success, to the deeper discussion of your purpose, you begin to shift away from the professional to the personal.

Your purpose can end up being the means to dovetail the personal and professional aspects of your life as you build your legacy. Still, you can get so focused on one aspect of your purpose that you end up in a position where you are getting in your way. When you work with mentors, their unique point of view can assist you in finding those places where you have impeded your progress.

Throughout this journey to determine your why or purpose, you have come to a greater understanding of who you are, the unique strengths you possess, and the ways that you contribute to the greater good of the world at large. All of this knowledge gives you the tools to understand what contributes to your legacy, and an inkling of the path that you want to take as you build that legacy.

Mentoring is a method found to be critical for those who are working toward achieving their greater purpose. Along the way, those individuals also become mentors for others who perhaps are looking to achieve and grow in a similar area. Essentially, as you look for guides, then you become a guide for others.

With that in mind, let's talk about how to set goals that benefit you and help you to grow toward achieving your purpose. Additionally, I will share some of the guidance that a mentor can provide in setting the right goals to meet your needs, and keep you on the path to true success in achieving your purpose.

Chapter 5

Goal Setting – Aim High to Reach a Higher Purpose

"Every single participant chooses to invest in themselves, grow, and ultimately help everyone around them to grow."
– Benjamin Franklin, 1706–1790

The journey to achieving your dreams and turning your purpose into a reality often starts by defining where you want to go and what you want to achieve. Once you have that in mind, then your goals and milestones are based on getting you from where you are now to that end point. Essentially, your goals become a map, one that if you follow it closely will get you wherever you want to go, and will help you to achieve whatever you wish.

Where I see individuals falter in terms of goals is that they fear the potential failure, or the fact that a complex goal with some risk involved will end up meaning they do not enjoy instant gratification. The challenge is that without risk, the reward is meaningless. Therefore, goal setting needs to embrace risk and potential failure, for the reward of achieving your true purpose, the one that aligns with your burning desire within.

For the next few pages, let us focus on how to set your goals in such a way that you will keep moving forward, instead of stalling out because your goals are not meaningful or geared to keep you trending toward success.

Avoid Low Hanging Fruit

When you are setting out your goals, it can be tempting to build motivation by setting up goals that are easy to attain, and ones that will give you instant results. The challenge is that these low-hanging fruit goals are the ones that can give you a quick dose of motivation, but over the long run, they cannot get you from point A to point B. Instead, you are likely to see so little progress that you eventually give up altogether.

Therefore, while you might want to pick some of those low-hanging fruit goals in the beginning, do not make them the only goals you set for yourself. Part of goal setting, to achieve a larger purpose, must be based around the idea of growth by stepping outside of your comfort zone.

What is your comfort zone? For many of us, it is the place where our strengths and talents have given us the most success. We tend to do what has worked in the past because it is comfortable and familiar. There is a saying, "If it is not broken, then do not fix it." However, the problem with that saying, when it comes to your personal growth, is that it means you are stagnating if you are not trying to fix or improve what you already are successful at accomplishing.

Let's take this to a professional realm for a moment. Perhaps you are in charge of customer relationships. You successfully meet the needs of a client, perhaps by getting their order out on time and without errors. Afterwards, you sit down with your team and start the process of analyzing everything regarding this client's experience. It is a review of all the aspects of the process, thus allowing your team to identify what worked well, where there were challenges, and what you ended up having to do to make corrections, even if the customer did not know what went wrong.

Afterwards, the information gained helps you to make changes to the process; and the next time, the customer has an even better experience, and your team functions even more smoothly. Why did that happen? Because you were open to looking for areas where improvement was possible, and then making those improvements. Innovation was welcomed to cure the issues and, as a result, future customers enjoyed a better experience, and thus maintained or increased their relationship with your company.

This example is meant to show how even when you are doing well, perhaps while you are completing the low-hanging fruit goals, there is still a chance for you to learn and grow, making adjustments as you complete these goals. Plus, there is going to be a moment in time when all those low-hanging fruit goals will be completed, and you will be faced with achieving or attempting goals with more risk attached; otherwise, your purpose will stagnate, along with your desire to achieve it.

Stepping out of your comfort zone will allow you to extend yourself, even if it means not being 100% sure that you will be successful. With that in mind, let's talk about what it means to aim high, and how taking risks can lead to greater opportunities.

Aim High and Take Risks

What is risk? Essentially, it is the chance of permanent loss, be it financially, mentally, physically, emotionally, or spiritually. Ideally, if you are taking risks, then you should be seeing the returns from those risks, even if the initial returns are just opportunities for you to learn more about yourself. Overtime, those risks end up rewarding you with the ability to reach your goals, actively engage in your purpose, and build a legacy that impacts others or contributes to the greater good.

When you set your goals, choose goals that inherently have some risk attached. Do your goals force you to stretch your potential and step outside of your comfort zone? Do they force you to look for ways to achieve outside of your current range of skills and strengths?

There is often the reality that we fear certain goals because they force us to stretch ourselves. We do not automatically know that we will be successful; thus, the fear of failure begins to raise its ugly head. That fear often keeps us from taking advantage of opportunities or experiences, ones that could accelerate your growth.

Outline your goals, and include risks. Embrace those risks because, even if you do not achieve them on your first attempt, you have the ability to learn and make adjustments. Failure is not truly the end, unless you refuse to try again, or refuse to learn from the experience.

Take one professional goal you want to achieve. Perhaps you can outline specific steps to make it a reality, but those milestones are overshadowed by an opportunity, one that forces you to stretch in order to take advantage of it. Instead of aiming high, you allow that opportunity to pass you by, and even though you continue to follow those milestones, you realize that the process is now taking twice as long. Your fire begins to fade out, even as you tire out because of the long process.

On the other hand, by taking advantage of the opportunity, you accelerate down your path toward your purpose. Along the way, you end up being exposed to more opportunities, and build a network that can benefit you throughout your professional career. Note that the goal of taking the opportunity is not that you are completely successful, but that you took the risk and were thus able to reap the reward in the long term.

However, before you can benefit from taking any type of risk, you need to understand if you are risk-adverse and why you might be that way. After all, there are plenty of individuals out there who feel comfortable taking personal and professional risks. They might even thrive on the challenge that comes from leaping outside of their skillset and learning on their feet.

Mary found herself struggling to take risks, fearful of failing because she worried that her boss would look at her negatively. Being unwilling to take risks, Mary was also missing out on opportunities, and tearing down her self-confidence. It also meant that professionally she was falling behind. Working with her mentor, she targeted her fear of taking risks. Using a few suggestions from her mentor, Mary was able to start taking small risks, which led to greater ones.

Her professional career started to take off because she embraced different opportunities. For Mary, a mentoring relationship was critical to assisting her to move forward and achieve her goals.

Others find themselves struggling to do the same. They pass up opportunities, not because they cannot see the potential benefits, but because the potential for loss looms even greater in their eyes. They opt not to move forward due to the risk, because they fear losing any progress they have already made.

In the financial world, these individuals are called risk-adverse or risk neutral. They might be comfortable taking small risks, but that can actually end up damaging their ability to progress over time. Perhaps you find yourself in a position where you are more willing to take risks professionally, but you struggle to do so personally. The end result is that you still end up feeling stuck, simply because if one area of your life is not progressing, then you will feel stagnant.

When I talk about aiming high with your goals, I am talking about being honest with yourself and finding ways to step outside of your comfort zone. Once you do, and have success, it will make you more willing to take even greater risks in the future.

What Types of Goals Involve Aiming High?

You know where you want to go and have laid out some goals, perhaps even smaller milestones. The goals might be easy for you to reach. Now I want to challenge you to choose a goal that is out of reach. It will make you stretch in one area or another. For instance, professionally, you might be wanting a promotion. Perhaps you are making efforts to show innovation, be creative, and work well with your team.

However, are you risk-adverse, unwilling to take on a big project, one that can showcase your leadership skills? Perhaps you see your leadership as a source of weakness. I have spoken about finding your "why" and focusing on your strengths. Taking risks can help you to shore up weaknesses and turn them into the strengths that contribute to your legacy.

So, let's take on that project. Be open to suggestions from others. Allow the opportunity and the risk to help you grow professionally. Tap into your team's strengths, demonstrating that leaders can still make adjustments based on their team's suggestions, ideas, and experiences.

Aiming high with your goals is not only about taking risks. It involves stepping outside of what you find easy and comfortable. It means doing something that is hard or difficult. When you accomplish a difficult task or assignment, that result can serve to boost your self-confidence. Then the next time you are faced with a challenge, you will be more likely to step into that challenge, confident that you are capable of meeting it successfully.

When I work with different individuals, I find their levels of self-confidence can be all over the place. They might be extremely confident in their abilities, and be sure of themselves, no matter what the situation. On the other hand, there are individuals who have low self-confidence. Perhaps their opportunities to master skills or tasks were limited, and the result is that they find themselves uncomfortable with taking chances.

Instead of walking into the situation being sure that they can handle what is thrown their way, these individuals find themselves struggling with doubt and insecurity. As a result, they already feel as if they will fail, so they simply give up.

Did you read that passage and feel as if it struck a chord? Have you found yourself unwilling to tackle challenges, simply because you are sure that you will fail? Essentially, what you are doing is robbing yourself of an opportunity to build confidence in your abilities. You cheat yourself out of the chance to prove that you can accomplish goals and achieve your purpose in life.

Stop cheating yourself! Take the plunge, not knowing if you will be successful. If you are not successful the first time, then do not use that as an excuse not to try again. Instead, use it as a teaching opportunity. Analyze, make adjustments, and then try again. Look for opportunities to step outside of your comfort zone, knowing that those chances are building your self-confidence.

Along with taking chances and jumping toward opportunities, you need to shift how you talk to yourself. It is easy to shift into a negative mindset. Many of us actually talk to ourselves with constant negativity, in a way that we would never talk to our loved ones. If you would not talk that way to your spouse, your child, your parents, or your dear friends, then you should not talk to yourself that way.

Negative self-talk makes us less willing to try new things or stretch to those aim-high goals. Take the next few days and journal some of your thoughts, especially your self-talk. You will start to notice a pattern. If the talk is consistently geared toward the negative, then you need to make a change actively and consciously.

That means, when you start to talk to yourself negatively, you need to consciously stop and turn it toward the positive. Even when you do not succeed, your self-talk needs to be geared toward growth, instead of personal attacks.

For instance, perhaps you take a risk at work. While you do complete the project, it has multiple bumps throughout the journey. Instead of telling yourself that you are not capable of running a project, you need to remind yourself that the project was completed. You did achieve your goal, and now you can analyze ways to reach your goal with less hiccups.

When you focus on the negative, then you start creating a reality that matches your negative talk. Time and again, what we focus on becomes what we create. Therefore, your self-talk is key to creating the life you want, achieving your purpose, and building a legacy that contributes to the greater good.

Stopping negative self-talk involves consciously creating a new habit and a new way of treating yourself. Over time, your self-talk will shift from being negative to positive, and you will automatically talk to yourself in a way that builds up your confidence in your abilities, and contributes to your growth.

Now at the same time, your self-talk does not mean building up your confidence without being realistic about your abilities. It means that you are open to growth, while at the same time, you are confident in your strengths and techniques. Arrogance can come from being overconfident without having anything to support it.

Therefore, spending time in introspection can be a great way to improve your confidence as you become familiar with your strengths and talents. Even if you identify a weakness, then you can choose to use it as an opportunity to turn that weakness into a strength. How can you do that?

Mentors have experiences, strengths, and skills that you do not have. When you choose a mentor, find one who is strong in areas where you are weak. Learn from them. Instead of just accepting a weakness and giving up, choose to learn and transform that weakness. While it still might not be your strongest area, you can still make improvements.

They can provide you with practical suggestions, ones that will contribute to your growth in that area. Plus, they can help you to analyze your progress and determine if you still need more work in that area.

Aiming high in goals and in your life, means finding ways to take risks, to grow, and to analyze and adjust, but also to take weaknesses and move them into the strength column. You can do that daily, through your journaling, your self-talk, and opening your mind to new opportunities. Self-confidence helps you to take on risks, but for many of us, building self-confidence is not easy. It involves transforming how you talk to yourself, how you interact with others, and how you approach areas of your life that are not going according to your plan.

The truth is that we are always learning, growing, and changing. By taking risks, opening your mind to new challenges, and building self-confidence, then you can aim high and achieve more than what you thought was even possible. The fire within you will burn bright and steady. As I touched on in this chapter, your thinking is often key to your success and to creating the life and reality that you want. If your thinking is not where it needs to be, then transformation is necessary.

In the next chapter, I want to focus on transformation, how you can start the process, and how mentoring can assist you in this stage of your journey toward fulfilling your purpose and building your legacy.

Chapter 6

Transforming to Achieve Your Dreams

"Knowledge is of no value unless you put it into practice."
— Anton Chekov

The idea of transformation is about taking something or someone from their original state, and using that as a base to create a brand-new idea or way of being. When you think of transformation as a person, it involves taking who you are now, and using that as a foundation to create your best self to match the life you have envisioned for yourself.

During our discussion, I have frequently spoken about the importance of using your natural talents and strengths to reach your goals and achieve your purpose. When it comes to transformation, the process is about taking all of these strengths and talents, and building a foundation for your best life.

Fundamentally, personal transformation is about learning how to change your life for the better, and to create something meaningful for yourself. Clearly, if you are reading this book, it is because you want more for yourself and you want to demand more from yourself. The "something more" is quite different for everyone, but one thing I know is that it is not about fixing yourself, as much as it is about taking yourself to the next level of your own personal development.

All of us start transforming as children. Our teenage years and even young adulthood is about defining ourselves, learning who we are and what we are capable of achieving. That being said, even as we come to a deeper understanding of ourselves, you begin to recognize that this knowledge can only take you to a certain point. Perhaps you notice that there are aspects of your life that are lacking, be it your relationships, your health, or even your spirituality.

Transformation is about incorporating positive change into your life, and allowing those areas of your life that might be lacking, to blossom. While there are concepts based upon the idea of harnessing the power of your thoughts to create the life you want, often this is just a small part of the larger idea of transformation.

Personal transformation is the process where you draw what you want into your life and, at the same time, you clean out limiting beliefs and other aspects that are no longer serving you or may never have been serving you in the first place. Throughout this process, you come to realize how you are part of a much larger whole, which would not be complete without you and your unique contributions to the greater good.

Too often, our ability to transform and let go of anything that might be holding us back is not easy. Our natural inclination to avoid risk can also make us defensive about those limiting beliefs. Yet when you finally signal to yourself and the universe that you are at the end of any resistance or struggle, then you are ready to work with yourself, instead of creating unnecessary obstacles.

Sometimes that means we start going with the flow of life, instead of fighting against it. Taking a risk can involve not being in control, and just letting life happen. Clearly, the process of transformation is highly personal and unique to our life experiences, beliefs, and values.

Taking Responsibility for Your Life Choices

Part of any transformation involves recognizing how the choices that you have made up to this point have created the life you have right now. Where you are in your life is a direct result of your thoughts and actions to this point. If you want something different, then it starts by taking responsibility for where you are right now, and how you created your current reality.

Now that you acknowledge your contribution to your life as it is right now, then you also recognize that you have the power to make it different. You are the one who can take the necessary steps to move forward in a new direction, or you can make similar choices and essentially remain on the same path.

For instance, you might be dealing with a toxic relationship, one that is not healthy. While you cannot control how others act or react, you are responsible for your choice to stay. At the same time, if you believe that you can change the other person, then you are participating in the denial of their own personal responsibility. This realization of your responsibility also means you are now at the point where you no longer view the world from the perspective of a victim.

Now that you see how you are responsible for your life, then you can embrace the fact that change is possible. If your life is not the way you want it, you have the power to shift it and make it incredibly different from what it is right now.

Arthur's relationship with his father was a struggle for him. Although Arthur spent time doing things for his father and his family, his father constantly degraded him. It became the voice in his head, the one he heard over and over. Arthur doubted his decisions and questioned whether his efforts were worth anything.

A friend decided to recommend a personal mentor to Arthur, hoping it would help him to break the cycle of toxicity from his family, especially his father. Working with his mentor, Arthur focused on what he could control, which was his self-talk. He also started to remind himself daily that his value was not based upon his father's opinion of him.

Over time, Arthur was able to make changes in how he responded to his father's words and actions. It did not happen overnight, but Arthur was able to set up boundaries that benefited him. Arthur also limited how much time he spent with his father, limiting how much he was exposed to that negativity. While Arthur's father did not change his behavior, Arthur was able to change how he viewed the situation.

The next aspect of any personal transformation is understanding how your conscious and subconscious minds interact with each other. First, recognize that these are not two separate entities, but they are just two aspects of your one mind. Second, the subconscious is essentially the aspect of your mind that controls all the automatic aspects of your life. The beliefs that you have adopted become part of the subconscious. It also serves to draw to you whatever you are focusing on.

If you want to change your subconscious, the hub of all your habits, then it needs to be an effort from your conscious mind. Yet when you combine these two aspects in a positive way, they can lead you toward the transformation that can allow you to live your best life.

As Arthur did, you need to shift the thoughts you allow your mind to dwell on. If there are negative thoughts about you and your abilities, then every time you start to think that way, stop yourself and replace that thought with a positive one. As you do this over and over, you will retrain your subconscious, and shift your mind into a more positive way of thinking, and beliefs that serve you instead of tearing you down.

Principles of Personal Transformation

As you start any type of personal transformation, you have already accepted responsibility, embraced the idea of change, are willing to go with the flow of life, and have begun to recognize the power you have to shape your subconscious and conscious minds. Throughout these initial steps, you have been preparing for personal transformation. However, I have also found that as you start to make a transformation in any area of your life, there are some principles that come into play. As you read through these principles, look for ways to incorporate them more fully into your life, and enjoy the powerful results.

One of the fundamental principles of transformation is appreciating your success, which is rooted in gratitude. That can be a challenge, especially if you had envisioned being somewhere else in your life at this point. Plus, society is constantly trying to tell us that where we are is not good enough. Pile onto that all the bad news that seems to be a part of our social media, television, magazines, internet, and even conversations with co-workers, family, and friends.

When we achieve something, instead of appreciating it, we tend to discount it. With all the negativity surrounding us, how great can our accomplishments really be? The truth is that appreciating and celebrating our accomplishments is key to breaking through the cycle of negativity that surrounds us on a daily basis.

Another way to break through that negativity is to consciously turn it off. Disconnect from social media, limit your television viewing, and even pick a certain period of time where you will read the news, and then not read it anymore for the rest of day. Some individuals have opted for blackout periods, where they do not access their electronics. The result is that they give themselves a period where their mind and heart get a break from the negativity. Thus, calm, gratitude, and appreciation have a chance to take root.

On the other hand, negativity can drain our confidence and distract us to the point that we lose motivation to achieve our purpose or dream. The reality is that this book began by talking about the fire burning in your belly to succeed or achieve your purpose. Now that you have reached the point where you are in the midst of transformation, negativity can end up being poison, so limiting your exposure is key.

Not only do you need to appreciate your accomplishments, but be sure to share with others how you appreciate their successes. Essentially, build your store of positivity by sharing it with others. The goal is to get you to the point that you find ways to use your gifts to make a difference, instead of focusing on fixing yourself. Inspire yourself to do bigger and better things and to take risks. In the end, you are building confidence to make things happen in your life and to fulfill your purpose.

The next key principle is to recognize that your life is constantly full of learning experiences. As the year ends, for instance, looking back at what worked, and what did not, means you have the chance to identify life lessons and absorb them. Life is a journey, and there are plenty of lessons along the way.

While success might be fun, failure is the tool of true growth. Review mistakes and use that information to discover what to do better for the next time. Once you capture those lessons, then distill them down to a few memorable pieces of advice or lessons that you can carry with you into the future.

For instance, if you enjoy reviewing your year, then pick three critical lessons you learned during the year. Why is this the case? Because our capacity to learn at any given time is limited. Instead of trying to learn everything at once, cherry pick a few key lessons and implement them. Then move on to another small group of lessons.

At the same time, remember that when extraordinary circumstances happen, lessons are going to pop out, and you have the opportunity to absorb them. It will be amazing how much you shift in your personal transformation by incorporating the life lessons that you are gaining, month by month and year by year.

The third principle is to recognize that the right attitude and the right actions come together to achieve the results that move you down your chosen path. However, your actions are guided by what you assume to be true. Limiting beliefs can play a part in your attitude, which can impact your results.

If you have a belief about yourself that ends with you thinking it can never change, then that is a limiting belief, and one you need to get rid of right away. To start to shift a limiting belief, you have to recognize that you are the one who created this belief, and you are the one who can change it.

Then create a new belief that clearly matches to the reality that you want to create. Make it a positive statement, put it in the present tense, and give it a positive and exciting spin. You are going to have to repeat this new belief regularly; but once you do, it will eventually become a part of your life, to the point that the limiting belief simply disappears.

Finally, I want to stress how important it is to define your values and live by them. Think about different people in your life. Can you point out that gap between the values they claim to follow and their actions? Now, the reality is that you likely have the same gap. When you examine your life in light of what you believe and your values, then you will notice that when you did not live by those values, then you suffered. Our lack of integrity to our values can often be a huge source of our suffering.

Learn to shift yourself immediately when it becomes apparent that you are acting in a way that is not aligned with your personal values and beliefs. For instance, if you value honesty, then it is critical that you are honest with yourself about what you need and where you should be spending your time.

In the end, following these principles can assist you in your evolution and the personal transformation that you have begun.

Identifying Your Thinking

The world and society at large are focused on dualistic thinking, where there is only a right or wrong, good or bad, and true or false. The reality is that life is much more complex, so rich, that there are multiple ways to think about a situation and approach it accordingly.

When you shift away from this dualistic thinking, then you empower yourself to become more conscious in your understanding of why things are the way they are, and also how you can effect constructive change within yourself and your community.

By redirecting your thinking away from dualistic, judgmental thinking, then you come to a place where you are focused on inquiry, conscious wisdom, and the discernment necessary to truly understand a situation and learn. Plus, you gain the capacity to effect constructive change in various areas of your life.

The other amazing aspect of abandoning dualistic thinking, is that you then open your mind up to so many different possibilities. What you choose to do now is based on your conscious decision making, based on your values, not on the "good" or "bad" that you might have identified with in the past.

Another aspect of changing your thinking from dualistic is that you start to separate from your self-image. Essentially, you stop trying to defend yourself to others and simply allow yourself to live according to your values and beliefs. Thus, you are making conscious choices and navigating through your life from a place of self-sovereignty. Your own feelings and emotions become a critical part of your internal navigation system.

As part of this transition, you also begin to explore why it is so important for you to achieve society's definition of "good." It is a deep dive question, one that means analyzing your beliefs and the subconscious parts of yourself that are motivated by this idea of being "good."

You learn about the social definition of being good, right from the moment you are born. It is enforced by your parents, families, friends, and institutions, through verbal and non-verbal feedback. That feedback becomes internalized and ends up becoming part of your subconscious definition of "good" or "bad." Thus, you judge your actions from these subconscious ideals.

Your experiences and judgments, based on "good" or "bad" definitions, compound those definitions into your subconscious. You start to employ pain avoidance strategies to protect yourself from potential punishment and abandonment issues related to being "bad." The challenge is that we are programmed to need to be accepted, loved, and feel safe. Our interpretations and bias that result from trying to fulfill those needs can distort how we experience our reality. Therefore, when you step away from dualistic thinking and start focusing on your feelings instead of how other people judge you, then it can be much easier for you to find your balance and ultimately get your needs met.

Now, at this point, I want to share that the drive to be "good" can cause us to repress or suppress parts of ourselves so that others do not judge us as "bad." When you are able to let go of that need to be perceived as good by others, then you eliminate that fear.

With that in mind, recognize that mentors are not judging you. They are simply a resource that you can tap into throughout your personal transformation. While they offer advice and a helpful point of view, ultimately, you are in the driver's seat and must decide how you are going to interpret that information or use it.

Finally, it is important to be good to yourself by listening, accepting, understanding, loving, feeling compassion for others, and exploring. Give this gift to all the aspects of yourself, without any conditions that might limit those things. When you are accepting of yourself, and good to yourself in this way, then you are free to grow and evolve, thus embracing your personal transformation.

Understand that you have the greatest gift possible, which is the power to choose. While you cannot control other people or events, you can control your thoughts and reactions. The truth is that circumstances can change simply because we change our thoughts and points of view, and then act accordingly. When you change yourself, then everything changes based on that perception.

No matter what you want, make sure that you are clear about the direction and the outcome you want to achieve. If you do not know what you want to get out of your personal transformation, then you will never be in a position to achieve it. Having a burning desire to transform is not enough. You need goals, an understanding of how your thoughts, choices, and actions are creating your reality, and finally, your purpose.

The focus on transformation is about reaching goals, but also about coming to a deeper understanding of who you are and what you can create. Studies have shown that our subconscious brains do not distinguish between reality and imagination, so what you visualize is as real to your brain as the book in your hand.

If you adopt the identity of a person who has completed the changes you aspire to achieve, then your actions will start to match that identity. Your subconscious and conscious minds will work together to bring that identity to life. Then reality will confirm that identity and start a process where eventually that identity and those changes are complete. Thus, you have made a personal transformation. Yet once you start the process of personal transformation in one area, with these principles and ideas in mind, you eventually will start to see that transformation overflow into other areas of your life. If you are searching for stability and comfort, then personal transformation can be the way to achieve it without depending upon others. There is a freedom when you rely less on others for approval, because then you are more willing to take risks and really get the most out of your life, both personally and professionally.

With that in mind, let's move to talking about how transformation can lead you to your personal greatness.

Chapter 7

Tapping Into Your Greatness

"Do not be afraid to walk the path that you must go on,
just because you cannot see the end.
The path becomes clearer as you continue to go on."
– Tracy Allen

Your journey is one meant to assist you as you tap into your best life, one where your purpose, the internal burning fire, and your strengths and unique talents come together in amazing harmony. Many of us have struggled to reach this level of harmony, simply because of the obstacles that life presents.

Throughout these chapters, I shared with you how important it is to set goals, to build a deeper connection with yourself, and most importantly, to find your why and identify your purpose. As you went through these chapters, ideas and new points of view have helped you shift your thinking and bring a new attitude to areas where you might have struggled in the past. I even shared the importance of mentors throughout the journey to this point.

Yet with all of that, another critical aspect plays a role in finding and maintaining your best life. It is recognizing the greatness that you bring to the world, and embracing mindfulness as part of empowering yourself and thus allowing your greatness to manifest itself.

Personally, the journey of your life is filled with moments where your greatness shines: for instance, when you reach out to others and help them grow, and when you give to others, not because they can give to you in return, but you recognize that you are feeding and invigorating the goodness to be found in all of us by giving to them. Those moments when you stop and appreciate the beauty of our existence on this planet, and recognize how you are connected to the greater whole, is part of embracing and sharing your greatness.

As I mentioned, however, we all face challenges. What are your particular challenges? Perhaps you struggled to clearly identify your purpose or your why. You might be struggling with the consequences of past choices, making you feel as if your life will never be the way you envisioned. On the other hand, you might be fulfilling your dreams but realizing that your legacy and contribution to the greater good is lacking.

Whatever the challenge you are facing, my goal in these pages is to help you recognize that your thoughts, choices, and actions are powerful enough to shift your situation. Nothing is hopeless, and you are not in a position where nothing can change. In fact, change is truly the only constant in our universe. Even when we try to shield ourselves from change, or attempt to avoid risk, life tends to throw us into circumstances that force the issue.

You might also find yourself dealing with feelings of being stuck, or unhappiness that you cannot explain. Those feelings are just another method that the universe uses to communicate with you and let you know that you are trying to stifle your own greatness. Think about each time that you were uncomfortable and stepped outside of your zone to take a risk. What happened? First, you learned something about yourself and came to a deeper understanding of who you are and what makes you tick.

Secondly, you started the process of growth because you learned, analyzed, and made adjustments. Third, you deepened your relationships with others because they provided support and guidance when you needed it.

Eventually, risky situations lead to success. Taking the plunge allows you to drive your life into exciting new directions. Those new directions could end up leading you toward new opportunities to explore your purpose even more fully. All of this naturally lends itself to living your best life. However, that best life is always going to be in flux. Nothing that comes together perfectly is going to stay that way. Eventually, we reach a point where even if things are going well, change is needed to keep us moving and growing. Our purpose may not change, but how we express and fulfill it may need to change from time to time.

Greatness in your life is an expression of who you are, but I want to be clear that it is not wrapped up in arrogance or an unwillingness to listen to others. Often, those who are the quickest to boast of their greatness are the ones who are actually dealing with a lack of confidence in their abilities. As a result, they focus on acting in the way they feel will get the best results, without addressing the reasons behind their insecurities. If you do not work to cure these issues, then they will continue to sabotage your efforts to explore your greatness and make it shine throughout the world.

Therefore, if you find yourself focused on showing up others, or you find it challenging to listen and let others contribute, then it might be worth exploring why you might struggle in these areas. Perhaps as part of your journey to a deeper understanding of yourself, you will also discover the underlying causes for some of your attitudes and reactions in specific situations.

When you work with a mentor, their point of view can be critical to assisting you in identifying those areas where you might need to give some attention, thus allowing your unique attributes to truly shine as part of your greatness. Now let's talk about what is involved in defining your greatness, and what you can do to make your greatness shine even brighter.

What Contributes to Your Greatness?

Right now, you are doing something that is unique, and contributing to your community and your world. Yet most of us do not even realize how our choices, thoughts, and actions in the face of various circumstances are actually opportunities for our greatness to shine.

Still, you might be wondering about what greatness means, and looking to understand how this quality can be demonstrated in your daily life, to the fullest extent possible. First, let's look at how society tends to define greatness. Perhaps your culture defines greatness based on how well you are known, how much money you have, how successful you are professionally, and what awards, trophies, or accolades you have received.

Yet even if that is a culturally appropriate definition of greatness, it is not accurate to what I am discussing. Simply put, greatness is not defined by our society, traditions, or cultural expectations, no matter how much money you have, how many people recognize your name or picture, or how many people recognize your accomplishments.

You define your greatness for yourself, and that is not determined by how you stack up against others. All the praise from others will do little for you if you don't feel it and know it inside yourself. True greatness is made apparent through your actions and works, as well as how you impact the lives of those around you.

Those who embrace their greatness do not make excuses, attempt to shy away from their responsibility, or avoid risks to minimize the chances of failure. Fundamentally, your greatness is not dependent on the greatness of others or a comparison between you and your co-workers, family members, or close friends.

Why is it so important to understand that definition of greatness?

When you live in a constant state of comparing yourself to others and competing with them, then you put yourself into a position where you are constantly working hard to keep up with those around you. How exhausting that can be! Additionally, if you live your life in competition with others, or try to follow the path of someone else, then your clear vision of who you are and what your purpose is can end up becoming muddied. The result is that you might end up being confused about who you are and what you stand for.

Competition can also make you fearful of trying to achieve or accomplish your goals, because you believe that your results might not exceed the efforts of someone else. Instead, you fear being able to achieve similar results, so you opt to not even make the effort. Imagine how destructive that could be when you are working toward a goal or attempting to bring your life even more in alignment with your purpose.

Therefore, stop looking to define your greatness in comparison to others. Attack tasks in your life with intent, giving them everything that you have to offer. You might be the only one who knows how much you sacrificed to achieve your goals: the hard work and late nights. Yet all that effort and work can result in helping you to clearly see your greatness and what you are capable of achieving.

Building up your understanding of your own greatness often starts with honing your strengths, practicing new things that you might find challenging, pushing through obstacles, breaking down the barriers that might be keeping you from achieving your goals, and doing all of this knowing that it has everything to do with achieving your greatness.

Keep in mind, you might have to figure out what does not work for you, as well as what does work, to help you express your greatness more fully. Greatness is fundamentally the ability to achieve what you want in whatever area you decide to achieve it, and that your achievements demonstrate a level of mastery and excellence.

To be great, you need to live your best life on your own terms, recognizing that whatever you choose to achieve is likely going to align with your purpose and what you are here to accomplish. Stop thinking of greatness as part of your career or a one-time thing. Instead, it is a calling, a sense of confidence, and a willingness to work hard and dig deep into who you are.

When you embrace your greatness, then you are focused on utilizing your gifts and talents to the best of your ability. To be clear, there may be areas where you would like to excel, but the truth is that you might never be able to achieve a level of mastery. If that is the case, then be opened up to shifting your efforts toward areas where you can attain a level of mastery. Doing so will help to build your confidence and thus increase your willingness to explore your greatness to the fullest extent possible.

True Greatness Takes Time

Now that you understand what greatness is, and how it comes from within and not from competition with others, think back to when I talked about your why and your purpose. It was wrapped up in what got you excited, your obsessions, and what you have enjoyed pursuing in the past.

If you start focusing on these things, then you start tapping into areas where you might be able to make your greatness shine. Yet I want you to understand that even while you are exploring your greatness, it is going to take time to achieve a level of mastery and experience. True greatness is not achieved quickly, but it takes effort and long-term goals.

"It doesn't matter how many times you fail. You only have to be right once, and then everyone can tell you that you're an overnight success," said Mark Cuban, a famous businessman and entrepreneur. Note that to achieve your true greatness, you are going to fail, need to get up, and try again.

To be great and win in life, you need to be constantly learning and focused on your growth and your transformation in the areas that you might have identified in the past. Your assets, beyond your talents and strengths, are your time, your mind, and your energy. When we try to learn everything, then we cannot be a master of anything.

After all, realistically, how many things can you master in one lifetime? You need to identify what your one thing is, the area where you are going to devote yourself to fan the flames of your greatness. Practice and devotion to learning is something you do, not only to let your greatness shine but to become even greater as you grow!

Distractions Can Kill the Spirit

Throughout your journey, you have likely realized that time is your greatest ally, and it can also be wasted if you are not careful. After all, when you allow distractions to sap away the minutes and hours of your life, then you are essentially trading your legacy and purpose for those distractions.

Picking up your social media, and spending hours scrolling, means that you are giving up opportunities to hone your talents and strengths, thus diminishing your greatness and what you can accomplish. To live your best life and leave a legacy that truly benefits others, you need to avoid those distractions.

I do not mean that you cannot relax by using social media or watching your favorite movie or television show. However, you need to give them the proper place in your life. After all, if you allow the distractions to take over, then you might end up filled with regret over what you were not able to accomplish, or how limited your legacy is.

Distractions also have a way of dousing out that burning fire within us. That burning fire often keeps us going, serving as motivation when it becomes challenging to reach our goals. However, if you do not feed that burning fire, or you allow it to be doused by the water of distractions, then you will find that it eventually goes out.

Eric was dealing with multiple distractions in his life. He knew that he was in a rut but was having a hard time figuring out what to change. His mentor sat him down and asked pointed questions about his priorities. Eric answered the questions honestly and found that the discussion helped him see where his distractions were coming from.

He started making changes to eliminate those distractions. Over a few months, his focus on his goals was resharpened and he started moving forward.

To avoid that, you need to set your priorities. These priorities can serve as a guide when you are making decisions about how to use your precious assets of time and energy. While you might have some overarching priorities that are present throughout your life, there are also the daily priorities that need to be clearly defined.

If you set daily priorities, then you are acknowledging how important your time is and spending it wisely. There may be tasks that are time consuming but do not necessarily need to be done by you. Consider delegating those tasks to others. At work, delegation can be easier to do, but it can be more challenging in your personal life. Yet remember that when you start each day, you need to have a clear set of priorities and what you plan to accomplish. Do not let distractions get in the way.

Part of your priorities should be focusing on self-care, giving yourself time to dive into who you are, what you believe and value, as well as how you can fully incorporate these lessons.

As we discuss distractions, I also want to share a simple but important aspect of greatness, and that is how your unique greatness impacts your connection with the world and the universe. You are a spiritual being, but if you allow distractions to keep you from exploring that spirituality, then it can dull your greatness. I encourage you to make time for all these aspects of self-care and growth, because doing so will help you to tackle any challenges, as well as continue on your path to achieve your purpose.

Along with recognizing the potential traps of distractions, I want to share how mentors can be key throughout the transforming moments of your life, as well as being a critical part of letting your greatness shine!

Let's talk about what mentors can do in different aspects of your life, to serve as guides throughout any professional or personal transformations that you may want to achieve on the path to achieving your best life, and aligning it with your purpose.

Chapter 8

Journeys Involve Multiple Guides

"If you can dream it, then you can achieve it. You will get all you want in life if you help enough other people get what they want."
— Zig Ziglar, 1926–2012, Author and Speaker

N o matter what stage you are at in your life, there will be a period where you might feel lost, unsure, and in need of guidance. Even as you move away from needing others' approval to be confident in your abilities, you will still find that your experiences limit your expertise.

Think about the last time that you took a car trip. Perhaps the destination is a place that you are not familiar with, and so you pull up your favorite map app and put in the address. Likely, it offers you a few options, so you can pick the one that fits your needs, either by avoiding tolls or construction on major roadways. However, once you select the route, you then listen to the directions and follow them carefully. Why? Because those directions are crucial to getting where you want to go. Without them, you will soon become lost, get frustrated, and perhaps even abandon your plans altogether.

In many ways, your life is precisely like that road trip. You have a destination in mind (your purpose), and you have several ways to get there (your goals). As you continue your journey, you stop for gas or snacks to refuel yourself or to make the best use of your vehicle (your strengths and talents). In the end, you still find that you need guidance from your map app. That is what this chapter is fundamentally about: finding the right map app (mentor) for the different aspects of your life's journey and all its many stages.

In case you have not already figured it out, a mentor is the map app that guides you throughout this journey. They can help you stay on track, and support you if you need to recalculate due to distractions or getting off track and thus making a wrong turn along the way. However, when you work with a mentor, that individual is not the only one you can work with. In truth, mentors are on their own journeys. Therefore, your mentor might have mentors of their own. Everyone's goal is to learn, grow, and challenge ourselves as part of our transformation.

With that being said, I want to dispel the notion that mentors are only available in professional settings. Too often, mentorship is based around the idea of career advancement, building skill sets, and becoming a better leader. While mentors can be essential in this setting to advance throughout your industry, they are also critical to developing your personal goals and purpose.

Our world is often divided into our personal and professional lives as if they are two completely separate entities that function on their own. The truth is that they are both wholly intertwined. Stop and think for a moment about your purpose. As you get a clear understanding of what that is, you are likely to gravitate toward work that aligns with that purpose.

While some individuals tend to believe that your professional efforts have little to do with your purpose, success in one is often critical for success in the other. I recognize that we have to do some work to sustain our livelihood, allowing us to care for ourselves and our families. For some, their work is just a paycheck and nothing more. Whether it aligns with our purpose or strengths seems to take second place.

That being said, I believe that mentors can help us find a way to align our purpose and strengths with a job that provides for our families. Again, it is about acknowledging how these intertwine, and then finding the right balance to fit your needs.

Let's explore how mentoring can be a critical aspect of all areas of your life, from your romantic and personal relationships, to how you interact with co-workers and progress in your career.

Using the Guide to Transform Your Relationships

My favorite example of this type of mentorship actually can be traced to traditions throughout the world. The idea of a matchmaker is woven throughout history, and that individual is essentially a mentor of romantic relationships. Serving as a guide, they learn about the different individuals. Based on their personalities, they then make recommendations.

It requires a level of communication and intuition, but also a keen level of observation. Perhaps your romantic life is not quite going to plan. Your relationships up to this point might have fizzled out for one reason or another. While it might appear that each relationship ended for entirely different reasons, a romantic mentor can often pinpoint where you might consistently be following the same path.

Mentoring also provides a natural guide to assist you in other relationships. Truthfully, when you are in the midst of a relationship, you can find it challenging to deal with specific communication tests or address toxic behaviors. The beauty of mentors is that they are not emotionally invested, and so they can bring a clear-headed point of view to the situation.

If you are unsure how to approach someone to mentor you in personal relationships, consider reaching out to a counselor or therapist. With a unique perspective, they can help you pinpoint where you might be allowing your thoughts and emotions to get in the way of your best judgment.

Not only that, but they can also be a great help in diving deeper into who you are, why you have specific beliefs, and how you might be sabotaging yourself in a variety of ways. For instance, you might be choosing friends that consistently violate your boundaries. By taking the time for guided exploration, your counselor or mentor can be a crucial part of determining why you allow them to violate your boundaries consistently, or why you make self-defeating decisions. That will involve diving into your past and understanding the foundation of your current set of beliefs and values. Not all of us healthily formed our values and beliefs. The truth is that childhood experiences or trauma could have made us focus on beliefs and ideas that limit us, even though the goal is to protect ourselves.

For instance, perhaps your parents struggled to put food on the table. Some nights, there was not enough for you to eat. Later in life, you might prioritize finishing all the food on your plate or always having a full refrigerator. Those habits become so ingrained that you do not even realize what might be fueling these choices. A more in-depth examination of this reaction can lead to your belief and the underlying circumstances. Then you can decide if this belief still aligns with your lifestyle, or if you want to embrace a different point of view.

Notice that all of this effort can give you the ability to better align your goals and purpose with your beliefs and values. The ultimate result is that you live your best life because you are getting to the heart of who you are as an individual, beyond what you want to accomplish.

Getting to Know Yourself

This stage of personal transformation and growth involves diving deeply into your subconscious and gaining a more profound knowledge of how you function and make your decisions. Mentoring is often a way to begin this process because they can break through the walls and bring a different perspective.

When you are trying to learn more about yourself, it can be challenging to be objective about your behaviors, emotions, and thought processes. Some individuals find that taking time to calm their minds daily helps them center and separate their feelings from their actions.

Do you take the time for quiet reflection and calm regularly? If you find your stress level increasing regularly, but you are not taking time for yourself, you will eventually become worn out. If you are worn out, it is hard to give your best effort to achieve your goals. During my mentoring sessions, there is a focus on how you treat yourself, and on outlining goals and timeframes for milestones.

The two of them are intertwined in your ability to create the life that you always envisioned for yourself. For your self-confidence to grow, you need to understand how you make decisions, and how those decisions reflect upon who you are.

Jerry's Story

The journey for Jerry began with a break-up. After his girlfriend told him the relationship was no longer working for her and ended it, Jerry found himself wondering why every romantic relationship seemed to be failing. He tried to figure it out on his own, but Jerry was able to justify his actions and choices. One day, when Jerry was out with his mentor and discussing some aspects of his goal-setting, it came out that he had a goal of having a loving relationship and a family of his own.

His mentor pointed out some of the ways he felt Jerry might stop himself from achieving his personal goals. Jerry opened his mind to what his mentor was saying. Instead of instantly trying to defend himself, Jerry analyzed his actions from his mentor's perspective. The exercise was enlightening for Jerry.

When he looked back at his most recent relationship, Jerry recognized how he had prioritized his career and put time together in second place. He also noticed how his listening habits and trying to multi-task could have made her feel like less of a priority. While Jerry did not expect his mentor to give him this guidance, he was grateful because it helped him to understand the impact of his choices.

Months later, when he met his current girlfriend, Jerry consciously prioritized the relationship and opted not to repeat his previous actions. The relationship flourished, and Jerry felt himself at peace. He was not shortchanging his personal life for his career anymore, and the result was that he felt successful in all areas of his life.

Did you notice that when Jerry evaluated himself on his own, he did not come to the same conclusions as he did when the mentor was involved? The truth is that I have seen this happen to others. Their time with a mentor, and a fresh perspective, is critical to their ability to make real change.

Are you finding yourself taking the time for yourself but coming to the same conclusions every single time? Perhaps it is time for you to step into a mentor relationship, focusing on your personal development. Throughout these chapters, you have seen how mentors can be a critical part of this process. They provide more than just a new perspective. These mentors also give you the benefit of their experiences and wisdom. If you are dealing with relationship challenges, they might share their challenges and how they overcame them.

When you hear that they also dealt with those challenges or issues, it can help you appreciate that you can get through this issue. Remember, mentors are that map app, giving you the options of different ways to reach your goals or address your personal challenges.

Relationships can often feel as if they are the beginning and end of everything. When one is not going according to your plan, then it can feel as if you are failing. The relationship's challenges color every aspect of your life. It can impact your mood and creep into your other relationships, work, and even how you feel about yourself.

Pulling out of that funk can be difficult. The help of others can be critical to remind you that this situation is not the end of the world, and you will survive it. Mentors can also be a reminder of that. Their experiences often end up matching our own. Thus, you see how they moved past these challenges and built a life they enjoy.

Notice that I focused on the challenges and then how mentoring can benefit you during these challenging times. I am not covering all the ways you can tap into your mentors' knowledge, but as you can see, there are many different times that they can step in, and you will benefit.

Mentoring Throughout Your Life

There are multiple areas of your life where mentors can provide benefits. Yet you might also wonder if it is possible to have numerous mentors at the same time. The truth is that mentors can step into different areas of your life and even overlap. At any given time, you might have a professional mentor, a personal mentor, and someone who is helping you dive into your subconscious on a deeper level.

Imagine three mentors at the same time! Each of them will be sharing their wisdom and advice, but the best part is that if you get advice from one mentor regarding your professional life, it does not mean you cannot apply it in a challenging relationship.

It is also possible that you will outgrow a mentor because, as you achieve goals and milestones, you will be looking for new mentors to reflect on the next stage of your journey. Gaining new mentors and letting go of others does not mean that you do not respect or have gratitude for past mentors. The point of shifting mentors implies that you are growing as a person.

Since this journey involves growth that can lead to personal transformation, you might be surprised at how changes on a professional level impact your personal life and vice versa. Multiple mentors can serve to accelerate that process. Therefore, be open to growing mentor relationships and allowing them to come and go in a reflection of where you are in the moment.

I also would encourage you to open your mind and heart to serve as a mentor for others. Even when you are still being mentored, there are plenty of opportunities to share what you are learning with others. Lessons that we teach others tend to stick with us even more, so when you share what your mentors taught you, they are even profoundly ingrained in you.

This chapter is meant to encourage you to embrace mentoring throughout all the stages of your life. I shared stories and examples intended to give you practical tips on putting mentoring to work in your life.

Now that being said, the next chapter focuses on how you can make the most out of every mentoring relationship. After all, the first assumption is that you are following the mentor's lead, and there is little discussion regarding how the mentee impacts the success of this relationship. Let's dive into how you positively contribute and make the mentoring relationship even more beneficial for you both.

With that in mind, exploring your role gives you even more tools to have success as a mentor and a mentee. Read on to learn even more!

Chapter 9

Maximizing the
Benefits of Mentorship

"Pursue some path, however narrow and crooked,
in which you can walk with love and reverence."
— Henry David Thoreau

Throughout these past few chapters, I have shared how mentoring can be a key asset throughout your journey, as well as serving as a guide throughout any personal or professional transformations. There are many benefits to reaching out for mentors, personal growth, addressing challenging relationships, or even just aligning your career with your purpose.

Mentors can come in the form of books, audiotapes, or webinars, as well as personal relationships built over time. Many of you will likely end up using a combination of these avenues to tap into mentors for all areas of your life. No matter if it is professionally or personally, mentoring can be the critical aspect necessary to assist you in taking a risk or making a significant change that you were fearful of in the past. Still, the benefits of mentoring can be limited if we do not take full advantage of them.

It is similar to being given all the advantages of money, education, and connections, only to opt to squander those resources and thus end up living in a way that leads to regrets and missed opportunities. On the other hand, when you are given opportunities and advantages that you use to the fullest, your life can be rich and truly meet your success definition.

There are several vital steps you must take in order to maximize the benefits of working with a mentor. Each of these steps also has the added benefit of increasing your communication, relationship building, and professional growth skills.

Start with an Open Mind

Perhaps you excitedly walk into a social gathering with friends, only to find that someone you have conflict with has also decided to attend. Your mind quickly shifts to all the reasons you have to dislike this individual, perhaps replaying the movie in your head of all their mistakes, slights, and horrible (to you) behavior. Naturally, you assume that their reason for being at the party with YOUR friends is one based on bad motives. They are just trying to ruin your good time and destroy your evening.

When you speak with them, you already have an expectation that the conversation will not go well, and it is no surprise when you both end up arguing yet again. Others around the two of you drift away, because it is embarrassing to be around the two of you at this moment. You see that your friends have melted away, and you blame that on this individual as well. There is no way that you can assume anything but a bad motive on their part. Eventually you leave, feeling frustrated, angry, and upset. Those feelings disrupt your sleep that night, so the next morning you are still blaming that individual for the trouble that you are now convinced they meant to cause.

Notice how you immediately attributed bad motives to the individual, and then your thoughts and actions brought to life a miserable time for both of you. Instead of assuming the best, you assumed the worst and were not at all surprised when that was exactly what you received. I would argue that you could have made different choices and acted in a different way to achieve a much more tolerable evening overall. Let's examine the evening and pick out a few ways that you might have done so.

First, your thoughts immediately went to past wrongs, allowing you to make judgments based not on the moment but your list of grievances. Next, you allowed your feelings and judgments to cloud how you spoke to this individual. As a result, they responded to your negativity with some negativity of their own. Both of you ended up creating the reality that you feared at the beginning of the evening. Remember earlier, when we talked about the power of your thoughts? This example demonstrated their power quite clearly.

Now let's stop and think about how you could have altered this situation and gotten the best out of it. That first step is to enter situations with an open mind. Avoid making snap judgments or assuming the worst of individuals. Do not be quick to get defensive and argue or make excuses to justify your behavior. Your mentor is bringing you knowledge and information from a completely new perspective. That being said, you have to be open to hearing it and giving the information some thought.

Too often, when we hear the advice and thoughts of others, our first response is to close our minds and prepare our defensives. Any criticism at all ends up being ignored because all we are focused on is defending our position at all costs, and justifying whatever we said or did.

Those who come with an open mind to a mentoring relationship find they get more out of it because they do not view what their mentor shares with them as an attack. Rather, they see it as a place to grow, to learn, or to adapt.

Stop and think about the last time you received any constructive criticism. How did you take it? Were you open to listening and weighing the information? Did you see how you might be able to apply it and thus see improvement in that area? Or did you instead opt to dismiss it right away, making excuses for why their advice or point of view was not accurate? Did you have a million excuses why you should not listen to them? Did you find yourself starting to attack their position or using other means to shut down the conversation altogether?

My point is that whenever you put up the defenses and close your mind, you miss out on opportunities to learn more about yourself. Mentoring is not always about ways you can improve, but it can also serve to help you gain a deeper understanding of why you react in a certain way, or why specific circumstances trigger an emotional response from you.

Therefore, if you want to get the most out of any mentoring relationship, you need to come to the experience with an open mind and heart, ready to listen and weight carefully what is being shared with you.

Cultivate the Relationship

One of the biggest sources of confusion in a mentor relationship is that mentees tend to think the mentor is supposed to do all the work to maintain the relationship, and that they should take the lead. The truth is that for a mentor to want to invest their time and energy into you, then you need to demonstrate that you value them, their time, and want to build a strong relationship.

How can you do this? When you make appointments with your mentor, be early. Show respect for their time. Along with that, do not overstay your welcome. If your appointment was for an hour lunch date, then be sure that you do not keep them past that hour. Doing so will show that you value their time and effort on your behalf.

Other ways to cultivate the relationship involve defining what you want to get out of the relationship, and then working toward those goals with your mentor. Be open and honest with them about the ways you are doing well, and the areas where you might be struggling. Do not paint a rosy picture if it is not accurate. That will only limit the ability of your mentor to give you guidance that can be of benefit.

The point is that mentees are not passive. You actually define your goals for the relationship and then utilize the time spent with your mentor to gain the skills or knowledge that can assist you to reach them. I continue to believe that the better you know yourself, the more you and your mentor will be able to benefit from the investment of time and energy in this relationship. In other words, you get out of your mentor relationship what you put into it.

Keep in mind that mentor relationships are in a constant state of evolution. That means mentors might be a part of your life for a specific period before you move on to another mentor that addresses other needs in your professional and personal lives. Still, once you make a connection with a mentor, those experiences and discussions help you to build a bond that can assist you in navigating complex aspects of your life.

When I work with individuals, I find that the best relationships are created when my mentees are open to hearing a fresh perspective, and are willing to learn from my experiences. Building the relationship means not bringing a suitcase of excuses, or reasons why it is not possible. Mentor relationships, in particular, are ones that show you what is possible, and offer ideas and guidance.

One of the ways that a mentorship can truly benefit you is in your industry and professionally. Perhaps your goal is to ultimately run your own company. The time spent working in other companies and with mentors can be vital to giving you the skills and knowledge necessary to successfully run a business of your own.

In this area, I personally have embraced the importance of mentors in building my business. From Raymond Aaron to others, the goal has always been to build relationships and glean information from them based on their experiences. While some individuals see networking as the means to accomplish this, I believe mentors provide the means to connect with someone who has already achieved what you hope to accomplish.

I look to my mentors as a way to identify possible opportunities to achieve success. Often, the challenge that comes with learning from our own mistakes is that we waste time. Mentors point out the potential pitfalls and give us the knowledge to save time by avoiding those mistakes. Essentially, they are providing valuable, actionable advice that can be key in building a company or transitioning into a new stage of your career.

Earlier, I talked about the importance of defining your purpose and connecting with your why. When you know what that is, you can find the right mentors to assist in realizing it. Think of your mentors as the means to fill in the skills that you are lacking. While you are getting to know yourself on a deeper level, there is a focus on identifying your strengths. However, I know that you spotted a few weaknesses as well.

When you are engaging with your mentors, look for ones that are strong in the areas where you are weak. Their insights can benefit you in the journey to turn those weaknesses into strengths that ultimately will assist your professional growth. The advice from someone who knows where you are struggling can be incredibly valuable.

For instance, you might be strong in marketing and sales, but struggle in setting up processes for fulfillment. Finding a mentor who is strong in designing processes can be critical to addressing this area where your weakness could limit the ability of your business to grow.

A Mentor's Advice Is Not Law

Now, let's be clear. While your mentor relationships are a great resource for you, that does not mean you have to do everything your mentor suggests without question. The most important thing to remember is that mentor relationships provide perspective, advice, and the wisdom of their experience. You end up thinking about a situation or challenge differently.

The role of your mentors is to provide you a chance to reflect, not to necessarily give you the answers or take away your need to make a decision. Real mentorship is about teaching you how to ask the right questions and shift your perspective.

One of the best ways to enter any mentor relationship is from the perspective that everyone you meet has something to teach you, and that there are learning opportunities around every corner. Mentoring relationships are learning experiences on steroids. With every meeting or conversation, with this open-minded perspective, you will collect a number of informal mentors throughout your journey.

As I mentioned in Chapter 8, mentors are not limited to just a professional setting. Plus, even in the professional setting, you are not limited to just one mentor at a time. Identify potential mentors that have experience with your goals and also assist you in addressing those weaknesses you identified.

Diversity of mentorship can also bring you a variety of points of view and wisdom for whatever challenges you might face. How can you make the most of these diverse and sometimes contradictory points of view and experiences? First, be openminded. Listen to what they have to say, and recognize that there are multiple solutions to address the challenges facing you, either personally or professionally.

Truthfully, there is no one right way to achieve your goals. Have confidence that the information and knowledge you are getting from your mentors allows you to shape your thinking about creating your path. No matter how you choose to achieve your goals, recognize that your mentors can be a great way to find those alternative routes by being a trusted source of counsel.

The problem for many of us is that we tend to get stuck in a way of thinking that is based upon a black and white choice, with only two options available. The truth is that no problem or challenge you face is limited to just two choices. For instance, you might be facing an issue with your child not following through with their chores. It might appear that you are faced with one or two choices to get through to your child, but the truth is that there are multiple ways to address this challenge.

Mentors are often a great way to get exposed to fresh ideas that help you see those other options. One of the aspects you need to remember is that if there are only two options, and both of them are bad, then you need to keep looking for another solution until you find the right one.

When it comes down to getting the most out of any mentoring relationship, there are several key take-aways for you to keep in mind:

- Select your mentor thoughtfully. Do not just pick someone because you admire their career.
- Establish the framework of the relationship and define the goals, as well as your expectations.
- Be willing to work at the relationship and contribute energy and effort. Do not expect your mentor to do all the work without any input from you.
- Be prepared with specific questions, areas where you want to get their feedback, and any requests you might have for support.

Ultimately, mentorship is not a one-way street where you are the only one who benefits. In fact, stepping up to mentor others, even while you are being mentored, means that you are spending time getting a greater understanding of others. Mentoring also helps to keep your mind young and sharp. Successful people not only have mentors of their own, but they also are open to mentoring others. It is a way to connect with your excellence and share it with others.

For me, mentoring has always been about sharing necessary tools for personal transformation, as well as capitalizing on your strengths to achieve your dreams and goals. At the beginning of this book, I talked about how you have a burning fire to achieve your dreams, but you might not know how to keep that fire burning or how to achieve those dreams. Mentoring is truly the means to do just that.

With that in mind, let's talk about how you can begin to actively seek out mentorship opportunities with your goals, purpose, and dreams in mind.

Chapter 10

Building Your Future With Quality Mentoring Relationships

"An interesting journey never follows a straight path."
– Marjan Van Den Belt

N o matter how challenging it can be, pursuing a dream is worth all the effort and energy contributed to the process. Along the way, many individuals can contribute to your unique journey. In many ways, those contributions are vital to any success that you achieve. While it might be easy to say that you worked hard for something, the truth is that no one is an island. All of us depend on community and relationships based on connection to fulfill our dreams and goals.

Part of the reason I have stepped into the arena of mentoring is that I see it as a significant way to build a supportive network of relationships. When I work with different individuals as mentors, I see their strengths and understand what they are passionate about achieving. Their internal fire can be intense but lacking direction. For others, they have the motivation and an overall goal but are struggling on how to reach that endpoint. Others can be dealing with obstacles and a self-limiting point of view that keeps them from reaching their goals.

Regardless of their situation or where they are in their personal or professional lives, I expect to provide a fresh perspective, help them find their purpose, and guide them on a journey toward a deeper understanding of who they are and what they can achieve. Think of all the areas we have covered and explored from the standpoint of mentoring. While each individual's journey is unique to them, the truth is that all of us can benefit from reaching out to mentors.

No matter what the case, you can tap into the expertise of others. It can be easy to believe that you are an island that does not need help from anyone. Yet, time and time again, experience has shown that humans are most successful when we tap into our community and build reciprocal relationships. While friends and family can provide us support and understanding, a mentor relationship is more formal and offers quality and measurable benefits. Therefore, it is worth the effort to connect with various mentors, either focusing on professional development and advancement or personal transformation and fulfillment. The nice aspect of mentoring is that you do not need to be pigeon-holed to just one area of your life. Multiple mentors can be contributing to your life at any given point in time.

Never assume that just because of your desire to make improvements professionally, it blocks you from making personal changes in relationships or your thought processes. Embracing the fact that you can create your reality based on your thoughts and actions can be incredibly empowering. However, to visualize what your life could look like, it can be incredibly beneficial to work with a mentor and see what the finished project would be like. Think of how you define success. Can you find a mentor who has already achieved what you hope for your own life?

Doing so can help you visualize the path toward achieving the future you have dreamed of building. I am amazed how often you can have a great dream or vision of your life, but time goes by, and you are no closer to achieving that dream.

Those roadblocks and distractions come up frequently. Our lives are geared toward a sense that if we are not busy, we must not achieve anything. However, being busy continually does not mean that you are making progress. The reality is that you are just filling time. Therefore, by being focused on a goal and deciding how to reach a goal effectively, you have a sense of purpose. Mentoring can be a great way to help you examine if what you are doing now is simply a distraction or is contributing to your progress.

Jenny's Story

Jenny had reached out to her current mentor because of some challenges in her professional life. She received the extra education required to advance, but despite all that effort, Jenny was getting passed over for promotion after promotion. The last job was based on the promise of upward mobility, yet now it seems that it was a false promise and felt like a dead-end.

That was when Jenny decided to look for a mentor. It was clear that her viewpoint regarding how to move up was limited. However, she needed to find the right mentor. With that in mind, Jenny looked for a mentor that already had the position she wanted. Oddly enough, that individual happened to be at a company Jenny had applied for in the past.

Jenny got up her courage and approached this individual. She said yes to becoming a mentor, and offered Jenny some critical guidance during their first meeting. They set a schedule to meet every two weeks, outlining small goals that Jenny could complete during that timeframe. Her mentor also shared parts of her journey, giving Jenny a glimpse of what was possible and what she would have to achieve to have that future.

Over the next few years, Jenny was able to change positions and get back on track. She built a more extensive network and connected with other individuals in the industry. That led to opportunities that hadn't been available in the past. Jenny could look back and see how her previous position had limited her ability to grow her network and build the right connections.

Years later, Jenny had her dream job and was now mentoring several individuals herself. She still touched base with her mentor from time to time, and it had become a warm and supportive friendship. What had started due to her career frustration, led Jenny down a path of growth and knowledge, and allowed her to build a legacy of sharing wisdom with others. Mentoring had indeed been a fantastic experience for Jenny!

Along with all these discussions about managing your time to achieve your goals successfully, there is also a need to check your judgments. Turning off our assumptions and judgments is often the necessary step needed to take in what a mentor has to offer. By being open-minded, you can take in different points of view without immediately dismissing their suggestions. I point this out because the reality is that often we can end up being our worst enemy when it comes to learning and growing. The tendency is to include excuses, and focus on why any suggestions will not work. Shifting that thought process takes conscious effort, but the results are definitely worth the effort.

Chapter 9 focused on how important it is to bring the right attitude to any mentoring relationship, and what you can do to maximize the benefits of being part of that type of relationship. Working with me, I encourage my mentees to give me a clear vision of what they want to achieve and what they hope to learn. There is something incredibly empowering about sharing your thoughts and being honest with your mentor right from the start.

If you are both on the same page, it can result in more benefits for everyone involved. Remember, this is not about what you get out of the relationship, but what you can give as well. From time to time, you and your mentor can reassess how the situation is going, and what you might need to adjust to improve the relationship. It might also end in you both realizing that this mentoring relationship has gone as far as it can go, and now it is time for you to move on to your next mentor.

Maggie's Story

Maggie had been successful professionally, but she struggled to maintain personal relationships. People tended to see her as unapproachable or abrupt. While Maggie wanted to deepen relationships with those in her personal life, she was unsure how to change her approach. It felt as if she was continually misreading people and their responses, which meant her answer did not necessarily fit the situation.

A dear friend reached out and suggested a mentor that might be able to help. Maggie was hesitant but decided to meet with the mentor and share her challenge. The mentor made her feel right at ease and even shared a few suggestions. For Maggie, it meant being open-minded, which was not easy for her to do. She even suggested the reasons why her mentor's ideas would not work. Yet, with the urging of her friend and the mentor, she set a timeframe and forced herself to give it a try.

After the first two weeks of trying those suggestions, Maggie started feeling more confident. It felt better. Some of the mentor's ideas, she opted not to try because it felt fake and out of character. The nice thing was that as her relationship with her mentor grew, Maggie saw the benefits of what her mentor offered.

Now, there are still moments when Maggie does react the way that she used to, but those situations happen less frequently. Being open-minded was key to meeting her goals. However, Maggie also found that the mentorship gave her ideas for other areas of her life, even professionally, where she felt things were going well. Their get-togethers were less formal, and the best part was that a friendship grew between the two of them.

Ultimately, the benefits of mentoring allowed Maggie to feel more at ease in her skin and understand herself better.

Add a Mentor to Your Toolbox

I shared these two stories to show how mentoring can benefit you in both areas of your life. It is also possible for mentoring to develop into a more profound friendship. These relationships can become two-way streets, allowing yourself to be honest about your personal and professional struggles, without a sense of judgment.

Every part of your journey will be focused on how you can increase your personal toolbox skills. What makes your toolbox unique is that you bring your experiences, knowledge, and strengths to it. Then you tap into mentorship, and suddenly, you can add other tools from your mentor's experiences and expertise. It also teaches you how to glean and learn from those around you, even if you do not view them as mentors.

Your confidence will only grow as your toolbox does. When situations arise that are challenging, you can reach into that toolbox and find what you need. If you find the toolbox does not have the right tools, the relationships built will provide opportunities for you to reach out to others.

Building these relationships is another crucial part of mentoring. You learn how to understand another point of view and incorporate analysis into your process as you weigh the wisdom and advice of others. That also means that you train yourself not to make snap judgments about others or the situations you find yourself in daily.

No matter who you are, learning from others, and being open to hearing them without putting up your defenses, can be the first step to breaking down barriers. Our world has been through some chaos in the last year, and divisions have become evident. We are all looking for ways to move forward that contribute and benefit our families and communities.

When you decide to spend time in a mentor relationship, you build a bridge and learn more about someone else. You also gain a better understanding of your beliefs and values. Explore the reasons why you believe what you do. Make sure that your beliefs and values still align with who you are as an individual. Mentoring can be a way to do that type of self-examination in a relaxed setting.

With so many benefits and opportunities, I encourage you to seek out mentors. Be open to allowing them access to all parts of your life. Do not be afraid of what they have to say, but listen with an open mind and heart.

When something drives you to achieve it, then all the hard work and effort are worth every bit of what you sacrifice and put into it. My wish for you is that your journey is full of memorable moments, that you capitalize on your strengths, and that you remember your purpose and legacy are being shaped by the choices you make today.

Let's define your purpose together and take steps to outline how you can reach each of the goals that will allow you to live your best life. It starts by connecting with someone who understands the mentoring process and can assist you in ways that fit your unique situation. Part of my work with various mentees is about defining what they want to accomplish in their lives, finding their purpose, and then actively working to capitalize on their strengths and talents to achieve that purpose.

For many of us, mentoring is about gaining the benefits of a fresh perspective, one that provide clarity, allowing us to let go of what might be blocking or sabotaging our efforts. It can also help us to identify things or relationships that might be dragging us down or draining our energy, thus limiting our ability to move forward. Everything I shared throughout these chapters was meant to give you a fresh perspective on how essential mentoring can be to your success.

If you are interested in sharing your mentoring stories, or learning more about how you could benefit, I would love to connect with you. For me, hearing others' experiences, and participating in the mentoring process, encourages me to continue being a part of the process of others. There is so much that I learn from my mentees, even as I help them on their journey.

May you find the right map and guide on your journey, and know that your choices and actions will serve to be a light for someone else.

About the Author

An award-winning author, mentor, and entrepreneur, Tunde Morrow has a gift and a unique perspective on people's lives and their success. She is insightful, open-minded, and able to connect with people easily. Her work as a mentor allows her to assist others to tap into their talents and unique capabilities to create their best lives. She loves to travel and see the world. Tunde is a lifetime learner and is always open to new experiences and adventures.

She believes and thinks in a positive way about people and life all the time. Tunde was born and raised in Hungary before moving to the United States, where she received a bachelor's degree from the University of Northridge, California. She is on her journey, achieving big dreams and living an abundant life. In 1990, she moved to Los Angeles, where she currently resides with her family.

Made in the USA
Middletown, DE
08 March 2022

62315395R00066